# HOGARTH

# HOGARTH

Neil McWilliam

STUDIO EDITIONS
LONDON

First published in Great Britain in 1993 by
Studio Editions Ltd.
Princess House, 50 Eastcastle Street
London W1N 7AP, England

Reprinted 1994

ISBN 1 85170 963 0

Printed and bound in Singapore

*Frontispiece: The Shrimp Girl, mid 1750s.*

# INTRODUCTION

'I know of no such thing as genius. Genius is nothing but labour and diligence.' This characteristically assertive remark, recalled from a conversation with the poet Gilbert Cooper, sums up much about Hogarth, the artist and his work. Its peremptory tone echoes the blunt, often pugnacious, assurance of a self-made man, proud of his achievements and sensitive to criticism. It is the voice of a man conscious of the part he had played in enhancing the reputation of British art and artists, and suspicious both of outsiders, with their pretentious theories and ostentatious ways, and of a younger generation, whom he regarded as all too vulnerable to the illusory attractions of an alien tradition.

Hogarth's voice, captured in snatches of conversation in coffee houses, taverns and artists' assemblies, is insistently one of empiricism and common sense, tutored in the school of experience and unyielding in pressing home the superior virtues of its own point of view. It is the voice of a figure described, with the dismissive hauteur which so enraged the older artist, as 'a strutting, consequential little man' by the American history painter, Benjamin West. It is a voice which it has seemed tempting to regard as the mouthpiece of an age during which there emerged a whole culture apparently as committed to the merits of 'labour and diligence' as Hogarth himself, a culture whose ideals the artist expressed both in his personal demeanour and pictorial output. By means of the receptivity of this culture to his moralizing scenes he rose, like one of his fictional heroes, from decent obscurity to fame and fortune.

There is a danger, though, in transforming Hogarth into a sort of emblem of his age. Like Hanoverian England itself — a nation undergoing radical change in its social structure, its economy and its international role — Hogarth was complex and contradictory in ways belied by his self-assured exterior. The bluff populist was also an artist of considerable refinement, marshalling an astonishing array of verbal and visual references in his work and vying with the masters, of whom he spoke so slightingly, in his efforts at painting in the grand manner. The aggressively chauvinistic little Englander also commanded a broad understanding of the latest continental art and could incorporate its innovations into his own work with considerable discernment and intelligence. And the unyielding moralist, with his fables of virtue rewarded and vice suitably punished, was also an astute observer, far from unaware of the shortcomings of Britain's emergent commercial culture and at times openly pessimistic about the developments he witnessed in politics and public life.

It was such a figure who enjoyed a success during his own lifetime unknown by any previous British artist. This success was built upon an appeal to diverse sections of society, as Hogarth carefully calibrated his work to respond to different tastes, exploiting a range of media and visual forms, from the vernacular languages of popular culture to the fashionable and refined diction of high art. In all of this, Hogarth, more than any other artist of his age, displayed a sure-footed sense of the deep divisions in national culture and was just as adept in exploiting the demotic tradition of the illustrated chapbook or street ballad as he was in making high-minded allusions to Renaissance masters or the classical tradition. Though the eighteenth century has bequeathed an indelible image of country house refinement, of the sleek urbanity of Alexander Pope or Joshua Reynolds and the aristocratic fastidiousness of the Earl of Chesterfield, this is also the age of the stock-jobber, the merchant and the 'cit', of Henry Fielding and John Gay, as well as of the murkier world of Cleland's Fanny Hill and the nameless hacks of Grub Street. Though he is often presented as little more than a sort of artistic John Bull — a straightforward, good-natured but ultimately rather buffoonish figure — it is Hogarth's great achievement to have worked not merely within his age, but across it, revealing its contradictions and exposing its shortcomings at the same time as he apparently revels in its sheer richness and inexhaustibility. This complexity gives the lie to any insipid moralism or debilitating parochialism, and continues to make Hogarth a compelling artist today.

The artist's early years were far from easy or auspicious. His father, Richard Hogarth, had travelled to London from his native Westmorland sometime around 1686, hoping to further his chosen calling as a schoolmaster, a remarkable — and ultimately injudicious — decision for someone from an unlettered rural background at this time. Four years later, he married Anne Gibbons, one of the daughters of his landlord in the lodgings he had taken near Smithfield Market. The couple had eight children, of whom only four survived infancy. Their fifth, born on 10 November 1697, they baptized William after the Dutch prince to whom Parliament had offered the throne of England in 1688 as a means of safeguarding the Protestant succession.

Richard Hogarth's intellectual aspirations survived his increasing family responsibilities. Soon after his arrival in London he had published a short primer on Latin and Greek, and in 1703 he decided to open a coffee-house where customers could converse in Latin. 'Any

Gentleman that is either skilled in that Language, or desirous to perfect himself in speaking thereof, will be welcome', he announced, adding: 'The Master of the House, in the absence of others, [is] always ready to entertain Gentlemen in the Latin tongue.' Surprisingly, this venture survived some five years before Richard Hogarth was declared insolvent and confined to the Fleet prison, together with his entire family. For over four years, the young William Hogarth was brought up under these difficult circumstances, though the family benefited from the relatively lenient regime in Black and White Court, where they were lodged from late 1708 until their release in September 1712. Six years later, Richard Hogarth was dead, and it is with some bitterness that his son, writing near the end of his own very different career, looked back on his father's life of blighted promise. Noting 'the precarious situation of men of classical education',[1] the artist writes with rancour of the 'cruel treatment' inflicted on his father by booksellers and printers, whom he blames for impeding publication of his *magnum opus*, a Latin dictionary, 'the compiling of which had been a work of some years'. It seems clear that Hogarth learnt much from his father's misfortunes, and his own hardheaded commercial sense and antipathy towards merchants and middle men, such as printsellers, stood as a clear legacy of Richard's frustrated literary career.

Shortly after the Hogarths' release from the Fleet, young William, now aged sixteen, was apprenticed to Ellis Gamble, a silver engraver of Leicester Fields, who was a distant family relation by marriage. This artisanal background was to shape Hogarth's career in a number of significant ways. Not only did the young artist, once he had set up in his own right, maintain the essentially shop-based practice of the independent trader, but throughout his career Hogarth also retained a frankly entrepreneurial attitude which contrasts vividly with the aspirations to learning and gentility cultivated by contemporaries, such as the portraitist Jonathan Richardson and the painter and architect William Kent. The technique

The Company of Undertakers

Beareth Sable, an Urinal proper, between 12 Quack-Heads of the Second & 12 Cane Heads Or, Consul-
tant. On a Chief Nebulæ, Ermine, One Compleat Doctor issuant, checkie Sustaining in his
Right Hand a Baton of the Second. On his Dexter & Sinister sides two Demi-Doctors, issuant
of the Second, & two Cane Heads issuant of the third; The first having One Eye conchant, towards the Dexter Side of the Escocheon; the Second Faced per pale proper & Gules, Guardent. —
With this Motto ——————— Et Plurima Mortis Imago .

Price Six pence

*Published by W. Hogarth. March the 5ᵗʰ 1736.*

Company of Undertakers, 1736-7.
*Engraving, 21.9 x 17.8 cm*
*British Museum, London*

*Company of Undertakers* (1737, see left) he adapts the coat-of-arms format to humorous ends.

For all his celebration of the conscientious apprentice in his later visual homily *Industry and Idleness*, Hogarth seems not to have been entirely happy with Gamble, whom he left before completing his training. In April 1720 he published his first independent work, an elegant shop card decorated with allegories of Art, Design and History, in which he announced that 'W. Hogarth, Engraver' was open for business in the family home in Long Lane. Over the next decade he consolidated his reputation, producing a broad range of works, from benefit tickets and shop cards to satirical prints and book illustrations, a field in which he met with particular success. By 1725 he was undertaking an ambitious series of large engravings for Samuel Butler's mock-heroic epic poem *Hudibras*, commissioned by the printseller Philip Overton, a project which marks his emergence as an assured and accomplished artist.

Hogarth had achieved this level of confidence partially through the training he received at the new art academy run in St Martin's Lane by the English portraitist John Vanderbank and the Frenchman Louis Chéron, who, like Hogarth at this stage, mainly worked as a book illustrator. Hogarth began to frequent St Martin's Lane soon after establishing his own business. In the fractious English art world, however, the academy proved vulnerable to splits and was obliged to close its doors in May 1724. By this time, the young artist had begun to frequent a rival institution which Sir James Thornhill, then Serjeant Painter to the King and celebrated for his historical compositions, had established in his home in Covent Garden. Apart from introducing Hogarth to the grand style of allegorical decoration, a field in which he defended his former master's reputation from hostile journalistic comment in 1737, access to Thornhill's academy also introduced Hogarth to the painter's daughter, Jane, whom he secretly married in 1729 in defiance of her parents' wishes.

that Hogarth acquired under Gamble was also to provide the essential bedrock for his subsequent development. Though many of the silver engraver's tasks were limited to the accurate reproduction of a preordained design (a constraint possibly informing Hogarth's subsequent hostility to the role of copying in artistic training), the young apprentice did acquire skills he was later to adapt to the very different medium of copper-plate engraving. Indeed, the importance of heraldic devices in the silver engraver's repertoire may have fostered Hogarth's interest in the use of emblems, while in works such as *The*

By this time, Hogarth had expanded his repertoire to embrace oil painting as well as engraving, and by the end of the decade had established a growing reputation in the fashionable new field of conversation pieces. These small-scale group portraits, normally displaying the sitters indulging in some form of elegant social interaction, had come to the fore in the 1720s as a novel, and affordable, means of recording one's family and friends without contracting the substantial expense of a full-scale work. The genre drew on Dutch and French sources, and had been popularized by the German-born follower of Watteau, Philip Mercier, who had begun to produce his dainty group portraits within a few years of settling in England in 1716. With works such as *The Music Party* (*c*. 1733, see right), in which he shows Frederick, Prince of Wales (whose Principal Painter he became in 1729) socializing with his sisters in the gardens at Kew, Mercier helped lay the foundations for a distinctive pictorial format which was to remain popular for much of the century. Native artists, such as Gawen Hamilton, Arthur Devis and Charles Philips, were not slow to realize the potential of this new genre in a market which had traditionally offered British-born painters few opportunities outside the relatively utilitarian run of portrait commissions. Though he claimed in his autobiography to have soon tired of the 'drudgery' that such work represented, Hogarth was too shrewd to pass up the favourable prospects held out by this potentially lucrative field. He had begun to paint around 1727 and by the end of the decade had made his mark as a painter of 'conversations'.

In many respects, Hogarth follows the conventions set by his competitors in the genre. His works are small scale (typically in the region of 2 x 3 ft) and display a grouping, usually focused on a single family, in some form of domestic or semi-public activity, such as taking tea, playing cards, making music or chatting, either in an outdoor or interior setting. At his most conventional, as in the somewhat overcrowded *Assembly at Wanstead House* (1730-31, page 53), Hogarth does little more than furnish his patrons with

The Music Party, Frederick, Prince of Wales
and his Sisters,
*painted by Philipe Mercier, c. 1733.*
*Oil on canvas, 77.5 x 57.1 cm*
*The National Trust, Cliveden House*

a rather stilted image of well-mannered social intercourse, with little sense of vitality or convincing interaction. On other occasions, however, he is far more idiosyncratically inventive, injecting an element of verbal-visual humour through the painting-within-a-painting which transfixes the attention of the male sitters in *The Fountaine Family* (*c*. 1730, page 51), or puncturing the solemnity of the hierarchically arranged domestic grouping by the mischievous antics of the young sons in *The Cholmondeley Family* (1732, page 59). For a relative novice, the conversation piece also gave Hogarth access to some prestigious clients — men such as Viscount Castlemaine, the politician John, Lord Hervey, the connoisseur Sir Andrew Fountaine, and the Master of the Mint, John Conduitt, for whom he produced the ambitious representation of amateur theatricals in high society, *The Conquest of Mexico* (1732-35, page 61). The modest size and relatively low cost of the genre also made it generally accessible to less exalted figures, such as the lawyer Stephen Beckingham, whose wedding in 1729 Hogarth commemorated (1729-30, page 49), and the conversation piece became widely favoured amongst the commercial bourgeoisie who were subsequently to represent such an important sector of Hogarth's market.

By the end of the 1730s, Hogarth's output of small-scale conversations had greatly diminished, though the feel — if not the scale — of the genre remains apparent in *The Graham Children* (1742, page 93), one of the artist's most substantial achievements as a portraitist, which provides a striking contrast with the generally sober representation of children in mid-eighteenth-century painting. While the offspring of the aristocracy and affluent bourgeoisie are generally presented as rather wooden miniature versions of their parents, identically dressed and adopting the same stylized posture suggestive of well-mannered urbanity, Hogarth strives for an illusion of intimacy and unselfconsciousness. The Grahams are portrayed as engaged in their own world, responding to each other in an apparently unmediated way rather than being displayed in regimented order for the approving scrutiny of the adult gaze. The sophistication of the work, in its subtle integration of allegorical meaning in an altogether plausible domestic setting, and the simple though effective composition demonstrates a mastery of the conventions of contemporary portraiture suggestive of far more than mere drudgery.

To some extent, this new level of ambition and commitment resulted — in a way altogether typical of Hogarth — from a belligerent sense of his own superior abilities. As his autobiographical notes reveal, Hogarth harboured a low opinion of portraiture as a genre and was dismissive of those who specialized in face painting. On a theoretical level, he endorsed the traditional disparagement of portraiture as intellectually undemanding. Rather than necessitating any invention on the painter's behalf, all that it took was a tolerably keen eye and a steady hand — attributes needed to copy one's sitter's features with the requisite degree of accuracy. No imagination was demanded of the portraitist, since 'their pattern is before them, and much practice, with little study, is usually sufficient to bring them into high vogue.' To make matters worse, the named artist who gained all of the credit and most of the cash was responsible for only a small part of the finished product. Hogarth, who always painted his portraits in their entirety, was contemptuous of the widespread practice of employing drapery painters to provide the clothing and backgrounds, while the portraitist himself completed only the face and roughed in the overall composition. It was this, he asserted, which was responsible for the pervasive lifelessness of most likenesses, and undermined the hollow pretensions of leading practitioners in the field:

*The little praise due to their productions ought, in most cases, be given to the drapery man, whose pay is only one part in ten, while the other nine, as well as the reputation, is engrossed by the master phiz-monger, for a proportion which he may complete in five or six hours; and even this, little as it is, gives him so much importance in his own eyes that he assumes a consequential air, sets his arms a-kimbo, and, strutting among the historical artists, cries, — 'How we apples swim!'*

This moral indignation was made all the more acute when the beneficiaries of the English mania for portraiture were foreign. The arrival in England of the French portraitist Jean-Baptiste Van Loo in 1737 piqued Hogarth's hyperactive sense of resentment, particularly as the fashionable interloper — whose flashy effects owed much to the unrecognized assistance of drapery painters — soon made inroads amongst the aristocracy and at court. Van Loo's overblown baroque style represented everything Hogarth most detested — and, indeed, his resentment spilt over into *Marriage à la mode* where, in the first scene (page 99), the profligate Earl's rhetorical portrait underlines both his bombast and his bankruptcy. Van Loo was, for Hogarth, characteristically and unforgivably French in the mannered artificiality of his work. He was thus not slow to proclaim his disdain both of this presumptuous competitor and of all who aped his slick and superficial ways. 'I laughed at the pretensions of these quacks in colouring, ridiculed their productions as feeble and contemptible, and asserted that it required neither taste nor talents to excel their most popular performances.'

When his bluff was called by fellow artists evidently exasperated by this torrent of abuse, Hogarth — ever confident of his capacity to outshine his colleagues — set to work on his most ambitious portrait, the full-length *Captain Thomas Coram* (1740, page 91), a gift for the Foundling Hospital that Coram had founded the previous year. Ironically, the *Coram* borrows much of its visual language from France, and a precise prototype has been suggested in Hyacinthe Rigaud's 1729 portrait of the financier Samuel Bernard. Consistent with his nationalist belief in native simplicity, frankness and good humour, however, Hogarth adapts his gallic model to reduce the distance established between subject and spectator. The somewhat shrunken scale of the sitter here, the affected negligence of his dress, the high skin tones and an approach to facial expression which accentuates particular details, rather than attenuating them in deference to an abstract notion of ideal beauty, all assert the essential ordinariness and approachability of the retired seaman.

It was such devices to which Hogarth returned in other set-piece portraits, such as *Benjamin Hoadly, Bishop of Winchester* (*c.* 1743) or *Thomas Herring, Archbishop of York* (1744), where a similar balance between dignity and openness was sought. The traces of France in the *Coram* were to prove a recurrent motif in Hogarth's portraits: Herring's likeness suggests a familiarity with the pastels of Quentin de la Tour, the seminal *David Garrick as Richard III* (1745, page 97) draws on the seventeenth-century history painter Le Brun, while portraits such as those of *Mary Edwards* (*c.* 1740, page 89) and *David Garrick and his Wife* (1757, page 133) demonstrate a sympathetic assimilation of French rococo. This highly ambivalent attitude towards other pictorial cultures — most notably to contemporary French art and the Italian masters — is a consistent feature of Hogarth's practice which transcends limited issues of stylistic influence. As we have already seen, and as we shall again have occasion to observe, Hogarth affected a pugnacious cultural chauvinism, shaped in large part by prevailing international antipathies and by the current fashion for importing foreign masterpieces, which frequently obscures what is in fact a remarkable cosmopolitanism in many aspects of his work.

This characteristic of Hogarth's art stands in striking contrast to the more vernacular popular prints, with their claim to documentary authenticity or knowingly mordant insight. As a shrewd businessman, Hogarth was conscious of the news value of a famous face. Not only did he enhance the topical appeal of his comic history paintings by integrating notorious contemporaries into his narratives, but he also had a nose for a scoop and knew how to exploit popular curiosity with a well-timed portrait etching. In March 1733, for example, he visited Newgate prison to sketch Sarah Malcolm, a young Catholic laundress who had been convicted of the gruesome murder of two old ladies and their maid. Within a day of her execution, which had attracted an immense crowd of spectators, the artist had a print of the murderess on sale which, at the price of only six pence, was designed to attract as broad a public as possible. This scoop was repeated in August 1746 when Hogarth travelled up to St Albans to meet the Jacobite rebel Simon Lord Sir

John Wilkes, Esq., 1763.
Engraving, 31.7 x 22.2 cm
British Museum, London

Lovat on his way to the Tower. Again, his commercial acumen paid off, and it has been estimated that sales of up to 10,000 prints netted the substantial profit of £300.

All of this stands within a well-established tradition of popular prints commemorating highwaymen, assassins and assorted miscreants — though it is a tradition normally serviced by obscure jobbing engravers lacking the range, respectability and reputation of a Hogarth. Slightly different is the artist's

celebrated etching of John Wilkes (1763, see left), the opposition polemicist who was arraigned before the Court of Common Pleas in May 1763, accused of seditious libel for attacking the king in his journal the *North Briton*. A former friend of Hogarth's who, as we shall later see, had clashed with the artist over his satirical print *The Times. Plate 1*, Wilkes had become an overnight celebrity through his irreverent defiance of the authorities and his notoriously dissolute lifestyle. Hogarth exploited Wilkes's public persona in a portrait print which combines satirical derision with apparent reportorial authenticity. As Wilkes later recalled: 'Hogarth sculked behind a screen, in the corner of the gallery of the Court of Common Pleas; and while Lord Chief Justice Pratt was enforcing the great principles of the Constitution, the painter was employed in caricaturing the prisoner.' The artist has certainly accentuated some of Wilkes's features, capturing the truculent swagger of his posture and lively, facetious grin. The eccentric parting in his wig suggests the horns of a devil or, more aptly, a mocking satyr. Yet more than a caricature (a term for which Hogarth displayed undisguised contempt), the *Wilkes* resembles a libertine portrait, such as the cheerfully blasphemous *Sir Francis Dashwood* (mid-1750s, see page 12). Just as the impious Saint Francis is crowned with a halo, so the liberty cap suspended from the Staff of Maintainance reflects a similar sanctity on the all too worldly Wilkes. The print — simultaneously allowing Hogarth revenge for a recent attack in the *North Briton* and tapping popular interest in Wilkes's notoriety — manipulates conventions of portraiture through subtle exaggeration and a clever addition of emblem, transforming the renegade journalist into a parodic inversion of the Liberty he champions, which Hogarth evidently suspects him of abusing.

The popular portrait engravings not only display Hogarth's responsiveness to the interests of a broad metropolitan public, but also reveal the essential modernity of his art. Though, like many of his contemporaries, he aspired to follow the most celebrated

Sir Francis Dashwood at His Devotions, mid-1750s.
*Oil on canvas, 121.9 x 88.9 cm*
*Private Collection*

masters in the grand tradition of history painting, his reputation was essentially founded on his capacity to engage with the complex texture of life as it was lived in Georgian England, to expose its weaknesses, satirize its follies and record its idiosyncracies. His appeal was rooted in the actuality of his images, an actuality enhanced by his use of reproductive techniques which not only delivered a wide and varied public but also introduced his works into contexts where they could form the centre of lively discussion and debate. The richness and topicality of reference in Hogarth's work, the familiarity of his settings and the immediacy of the moral dilemmas highlighted in his graphic

dramas ensured that his prints engaged his audience on more than the passive level of connoisseurship and demanded of them instead an active reading rooted in their experience of everyday life.

This level of engagement was most fully achieved in what the artist himself described as his 'modern moral subjects, a field', he adds with characteristic immodesty, 'not broken up in any country or any age'. His innovation was, as he claimed, to use painting and engraving as a story-telling medium in which credible fictional characters acted out moral dramas familiar in the modern world, dramas from which the viewer could glean valuable ethical instruction while being seduced by the image's humour and actuality. Though precedents for this narrative mode can be found in Italian and Dutch popular culture, Hogarth's great achievement was to lend his characters an almost novelistic credibility, enhanced by the range and variety of the settings in which he situated their different tales. In his most celebrated works — *A Harlot's Progress* (1732), *A Rake's Progress* (1735), *Marriage à la mode* (1745) and *Industry and Idleness* (1747) — Hogarth elaborated complex narratives over a sequence of images, though the roots of the genre can be found in such self-contained comic scenes as *The Denunciation* (*c*. 1729, page 45) which the artist began to produce soon after taking up painting in the late 1720s. These works combine a rich vein of popular imagery, often burlesque or erotic in tone, with a scenography reminiscent of the conversation pieces on which the artist was busily engaged during the early 1730s. The product of this hybridization is a tableau in which the viewer is invited to piece together a fuller narrative of cause and effect from the immediate evidence contained in the pantomime of gesture and facial expression stimulated by the incident portrayed.

A further ingredient in the evolution of the modern moral subject (or comic history painting, as it was also called) came from the theatre. Most immediately, Hogarth was stimulated by the success of John

Gay's *The Beggar's Opera*, a music-drama first produced to popular acclaim in January 1728. The artist's fascination with the piece, with its contemporary setting, its exploration of a marginal world populated by highwaymen and prostitutes, and its topical allusions to politics and high society, encouraged him to use its climactic scene (page 47) to pursue a virtual apprenticeship in the skills of pictorial composition. After almost a decade as a professional engraver, Hogarth had become adept as an illustrator of fictional texts, and it is this background in, and affiliation with, an essentially literary approach to imagery that shaped the form of the artist's own graphic dramas. For contemporaries, as for later commentators, Hogarth was regarded as the pictorial equivalent of the novelist or playwright. For the essayist Charles Lamb, for example, writing in 1811, 'his graphic representations are indeed books: they have the teeming, fruitful, suggestive meaning of *words*. Other pictures we look at — his prints we read.'[2] Lamb's observation, which led him to reckon Hogarth the virtual equal of Shakespeare, was based not only on the artist's persuasive characterization, but also on the density of reference which absorbed the spectator in deciphering the implications of the action fixed in a suspended moment of time.

That theatricality serves as more than a loose analogy for the method developed by Hogarth is made clear in the artist's autobiographical notes. Here, he speaks of his desire to 'compose pictures on canvas, similar to representations on the stage; and [I] further hope that they will be tried by the same test, and criticized by the same criterion.' 'I have endeavoured,' he later remarks, 'to treat my subjects as a dramatic writer: my picture is my stage, and men and women my players, who by means of certain actions and gestures, are to exhibit *a dumb show*.' There was nothing particularly novel in thinking in such terms, which are entirely consistent with classical aesthetic theory embodied in Horace's notion of '*ut pictura poesis*' ('as in painting, so in poetry'), set out in his *Ars poetica*. Where Hogarth does mark a significant

departure is in the fact that the drama is of his own devising. Rather than selecting a key incident from a canonical text — whether biblical, classical or modern — Hogarth made up his own narratives and told them directly in pictorial form. He did, of course, also pursue the more conventional route of borrowing from literary sources, producing scenes from Milton and Shakespeare, for example — both of whose works feature, together with Swift, in the self-portrait completed in 1745 (page 111). Yet Hogarth's sense of drama is more appropriately satisfied in the present day, recorded in all its anti-heroic diversity in the writings of John Gay or the artist's close friend Henry Fielding. Fielding's exploration of the narrative potential of the novel, a form vastly expanded during Hogarth's lifetime by writers such as Defoe, Swift and Smollett, is widely regarded as providing a further literary source for Hogarth's elaboration of characters such as Tom Rakewell in *A Rake's Progress* or Tom Idle in *Industry and Idleness*.

Hogarth and Fielding shared a conviction in art's capacity to instruct and to exert a lasting impact on the individual's manners and moral bearing. Again drawing on established aesthetic theory, both attributed to the sense of sight an immediacy and sensitivity which infallibly impressed the viewer with the moral meaning of the scene before him. As Fielding remarked in an essay on satire in *The Champion* in June 1740, 'the force of example is infinitely stronger, as well as quicker, than precept; for which Horace assigns this reason, that our eyes convey the idea more briskly to the understanding than our ears.'[3] The point is corroborated by Hogarth in his autobiography, where he relates it directly to the didactic ambitions of his own work: 'Occular demonstration will carry more conviction to the mind of a sensible man, than all he would find in a thousand volumes; and this has been attempted in the prints I have composed.' The structure of the *Progresses* was specifically designed to satisfy this morally improving intent, at least on one level of reading. As in a novel or a play, Hogarth presents a character who takes a certain course of action which produces particular consequences: a decision, attitude of mind or failure of will is shown, through dramatically inter-related steps, as leading to an inevitable (and generally unfortunate) outcome. Virtue is rewarded, and vice suffers just punishment — or so it may seem.

The literary quality of Hogarth's work is evident in a number of ways in the form and structure of his narrative sequences. In his first essay in the genre, *A Harlot's Progress* (see pages 20-22), for which only the prints survive, we can see the artist presenting his characters in a series of settings reminiscent of the theatrical stage — so clear was the analogy, indeed, that following the immense success of the prints the playwright Theophilus Cibber used them as the basis for 'a grotesque pantomime entertainment' at Drury Lane, in which each scene began with a *tableau vivant* borrowed from Hogarth's work. Internally, each print in the series tends to invite us to read it from left to right, in the same way as we would approach a page of text. Similarly, hints as to the passage of time are arranged within a print on this left–right axis: in the opening scene, for example (see page 20), the heroine's recent arrival in London from York is indicated through the cart on the left; her present predicament is embodied in her encounter with the bawd at the centre of the composition, and her likely destiny indicated in the figure of the client waiting on the right, who follows the women's conversation with particular interest. Like the chapters of a book, one episode succeeds another, each opening up a new stage in the hero or heroine's 'progress', each inviting us to imagine for ourselves the events which have occurred between prints — a process which Hogarth facilitates by providing visual cues, such as the mask abandoned on the dressing table in the second print of the *Harlot*, which suggests that the heroine has attended a masquerade the previous evening together with her lover, who tip-toes out in the background.

In his attitude towards characterization Hogarth also betrays a strong literary sense, as the artist himself remarked in his autobiography. Characters such as the Rake (pages 65-79) or the Idle Apprentice come to life not merely through Hogarth's ability to sustain a consistency of appearance in a range of contexts across a sequence of images. There is also a remarkably refined sense of what, in entirely anachronistic terms, could be described as a psychological appropriateness. In *Industry and Idleness* (see pages 23 and 24), for example, the miscreant Tom Idle is repeatedly shown in physically precarious positions — perched on a tombstone next to an open grave as he gambles in plate three, bobbing in a small boat on a choppy sea in plate five, startled by a falling cat as he sleeps in a prostitute's collapsed bed in plate seven. His conscientious fellow apprentice, Francis Goodchild, is characterized in terms of his association with closed spaces, secure and protected, such as the box pew in church, his master's workshop, or the elegant town house he acquires following marriage to his employer's daughter.

This subtlety of approach informed Hogarth's entire philosophy of characterization and helps him to develop such memorable figures as the merchant in the contract scene of *Marriage à la mode* (1743-45 page 99) or the prudish woman in *Morning* (1736-38, page 83). It is an attitude towards the portrayal of character which, Hogarth insisted, was based upon the careful observation of nature rather than the arbitrary exaggeration of physical features associated with caricature. The growing popularity of caricature sketches, introduced from Italy by the artist and dealer Arthur Pond in the 1730s, prompted Hogarth to draw a clear and public distinction between what he regarded as a crudely imprecise form of sketching and the careful, psychologically penetrating portrayal of the individual in which he excelled. The point is made in visual form in *Characters and Caricatures* (1743, see page 15), where Hogarth juxtaposes caricatures by the Italians Ghezzi, Annibale Carracci and Leonardo with three heads taken from Raphael and an array of male profiles of his own invention. His allusion to Fielding's *Joseph Andrews* in the print

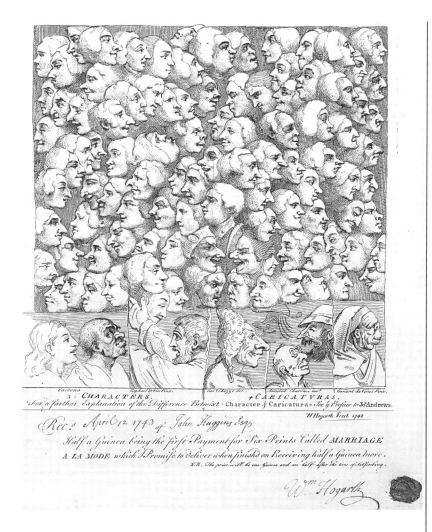

Characters and Caricatures, *1743*.
*Engraving, 19.5 x 20.6 cm*
*British Museum, London*

---

directs the viewer to a passage in the novel in which the writer explicitly discusses Hogarth's work, underlining the way in which his portrayal of character could be understood by contemporaries in essentially novelistic terms:

*He who should call the Ingenious* Hogarth *a Burlesque Painter, would, in my Opinion, do him very little Honour; for sure it is much easier, much less the Subject of Admiration, to paint a Man with a Nose, or any other Feature of preposterous Size, or to expose him in some absurd or monstrous Attitude, than to express the Affections of Men on Canvas. It hath been thought a vast*

*Commendation of a Painter, to say his Figures* seem to breathe; *but surely, it is a much greater and nobler Applause,* that they appear to think.

In the same way, just as a writer might describe the features of a room, or a dramatist stipulate specific props, as a means of giving us some insight into a character or incident, so Hogarth pays particular attention to setting. Like the Victorian narrative painters of a later generation, he uses furnishings, clothing and interior decorations to comment on his characters and their adventures. The paintings in the Jew's appartment in the second scene of the *Harlot* (see page 20), for example, speak of divine retribution, alluding to the heroine's own inevitable fate for having betrayed her new master. Similarly, in their haphazard and tasteless accumulation, the furnishings of the unhappy newlyweds' home in the second scene of *Marriage à la mode* (page 101) suggest an unease with domestic life which leads to the fatal outcome of the story. Indeed, commenting on the apparently inexhaustible quality of Hogarth's imagery, Charles Lamb remarked on 'the dumb rhetoric of the scenery — for tables, and chairs, and joint stools, in Hogarth, are living and significant things.' Like a novelist or dramatist, Hogarth also introduces subsidiary characters — such as the Harlot's maid — or even simple sub-plots, such as the story of the faithful Sarah Young whom Tom Rakewell abandons in the opening scene of *A Rake's Progress* (page 65). The effect of such devices is to increase the viewer's willingness to accept the realism of the tale, without detracting from the dramatic impact of the main story.

A further verbal device found in certain prints is Hogarth's use of a text — written either by himself or a colleague — to underline the action and its moral meaning. *A Rake's Progress*, for example, was accompanied by a verse commentary, while *Industry and Idleness* incorporated biblical quotations in the decorative border framing the images. The narrative quality of Hogarth's work, together with the profusion of detail and complex allusion incorporated into

Pamela and Mr. B in the Summer House,
*painted by Joseph Highmore, c. 1744.*
*Oil on canvas, 62.9 x 75.6 cm*
*Fitzwilliam Museum, Cambridge*

most images, further encouraged the publication of written commentaries, the most famous of which, *Hogarth Moralized* (1766-68), written by the Reverend John Trusler in conjunction with the artist's widow, accentuated and simplified the prints' moral content. This reversal of normal procedure — in which the image was subsidiary to, and dependent on a pre-existing text — underlines the inherent richness of Hogarth's imagery and the tight plotting through which individual episodes are inter-related.

In this respect, it is instructive to contrast Hogarth's method as a visual storyteller with the work of his contemporary Joseph Highmore (1692-1780), who in 1744 completed a series of twelve oils based on Samuel Richardson's enormously successful epistolary novel *Pamela, or Virtue Rewarded*, first published in 1740-41. Richardson had originally approached Hogarth in 1740, proposing that he should provide illustrations to the printed text. The project came to nothing, however, and it was only with the sixth edition, issued in 1742, that plates

were included, based on designs by Hayman and Gravelot. Highmore conceived his own venture much like Hogarth's modern moral subjects, producing a series of uniform canvases after which independent prints were engraved, with brief explanatory texts describing each particular episode. When viewed as a series, Highmore's images remain stubbornly inscrutable to any viewer unfamiliar with Richardson's narrative; nor do they cohere into anything resembling a legible episodic sequence as little is done to provide causal connections between adjacent scenes. In an image such as *Pamela and Mr B. in the Summer House* (see left), for example, we need substantial extrinsic knowledge to appreciate that Pamela Andrews, a virtuous lady's maid, is here repelling the first of a series of increasingly pressing advances from Mr B., her dissolute employer. Pamela's downcast gaze, suspended movement and restraining gesture, together with Mr. B's indiscreet, though relatively chaste embrace, sketch out the fundamental action, though Highmore restricts subsidiary detail to the interrupted sewing which lies abandoned in the background. When compared to a scene such as the opening of *A Harlot's Progress* (or the directly comparable narrative of *The Lady's Last Stake*, 1758-59, page 137), Highmore's work seems unhelpfully laconic. Where Hogarth secretes a multitude of detail, Highmore opts for elegant simplicity; where Hogarth channels our attention and forces us to elaborate a complex dramatic context, Highmore offers the spectator so much latitude in piecing together events that one is practically obliged to turn to his original prose source for guidance.

On one level, Hogarth's 'novelistic' attention to detail — his realization that apparently superfluous accessories or incidents could communicate useful clues, as well as encouraging us to accept the plausibility of the scene — seems remarkably modern. In another way, however, Hogarth's narrative technique drew on well-established devices of emblem, allegory and verbal-visual puns which by the eighteenth century had largely migrated from polite to popular art, notably graphic satire. Emblems had been central to the European tradition since antiquity as a means of providing physical form for generally abstract qualities or ideas. As fixed and formalized representations — often human (such as Britannia or Liberty), though equally animal (the dog as fidelity) or inanimate (the cypress tree representing the just ruler) — emblems offered the artist a sort of shorthand for translating often complex concepts into visual terms. With his elaborate baroque decorations for buildings such as the Royal Naval Hospital in Greenwich, Hogarth's father-in-law, Sir James Thornhill, was a leading exponent of the idiom, but this overblown visual rhetoric quickly lost favour during the eighteenth century. Where it remained vigorous throughout Hogarth's lifetime was in the satirical print, which blossomed in early Georgian England, initially inspired by Dutch precedent.

Hogarth himself provides a typical example of the form in one of his earliest independent works, *The South Sea Scheme* (1721, see page 37), an engraving he published in 1721 in response to the financial scandal of the South Sea Bubble. This apparently surreal accumulation of city merchants, partially clothed figures, animals and demons comes into focus (with the help of a satirical verse and explanatory key) once the viewer approaches the scene not as a naturalistic representation but as an allegory in which particular figures are to be read as embodying specific qualities or ideas. We thus learn that the naked figure being broken on a wheel is Honesty, her persecutor Self-Interest, while Villainy scourges Honour in the background. Through a cumulative process of detailed scrutiny, reading and interpretation viewers piece together the overall meaning of the print, rather as they would solve a crossword puzzle or a rebus.

Formal allegories are relatively rare in Hogarth's modern moral subjects, though in *The Polling* from the *Election* series (1753-54, page 125) he does infiltrate the figure of Britannia into the scene, while the gloves in the fourth plate of *Industry and Idleness* (see

page 23) are clasped in a symbol of amity. More usually, he devises his own ingenious emblems as a commentary on the action. In the first scene of *Marriage à la mode* (page 99), for example, the two morose-looking hounds manacled together in the left foreground prefigure the fate of the central characters, as does the goose whose head lolls lifelessly from Moll's basket in the opening scene of the *Harlot's Progress* (see page 20). Hogarth also favours verbal-visual puns — a standby of popular graphic satire — in which the linguistic associations of a particular object or incident trigger clues which add to the viewer's understanding. Again in the first scene of the *Harlot*, for example, we are encouraged to read the pile of buckets tumbling to the ground in terms of the (moral) 'fall' risked by the young country girl, while the stolen pocket watch which Moll brandishes two scenes later (see page 21) suggests that 'time is running out' as the justice arrives with his men to arrest her for prostitution.

All of this suggests an attitude towards pictorial meaning sympathetic to the playful, the witty, and the ambiguous — to a perspective on form and content which Hogarth celebrated in his *Analysis of Beauty* under the term 'intricacy', a value which he claimed offered satisfaction in every aspect of life:

*The active mind is ever bent to be employ'd. Pursuing is the business of our lives; and even abstracted from any other view, gives pleasure. Every arising difficulty, that for a while attends and interrupts the pursuit, gives a sort of spring to the mind, enhances the pleasure, and makes what would else be toil and labour, become sport and recreation.*[4]

This pleasure in the exercise of mental agility, in playing with rules, secreting hidden meanings and defying mundane logic produces the world-turned-upside-down of the satire on false perspective (1754, see page 18) or the playful stab in the back which the escaping lover apparently delivers to the Jew in the second plate of the *Harlot*. It is an attitude towards

Satire on False Perspective, 1754.
*Engraving, 20.8 x 17.1 cm*
*British Museum, London*

the image which conceives the art work as a focus for collective viewing, drawing upon the ingenuity of all concerned to winkle out sense and piece together a narrative as a means of fostering an involvement which is ultimately moral in intent.

For at the heart of the enterprise is morality, though morality conceived less as a cut-and-dried injunction, implacable and unambiguous, than as a challenge, a provocation to self-interrogation and to taking a stand. On one level, of course, Hogarth's morals seem as black and white as the engravings he uses to recount his tales of vice and virtue, of material success and spiritual perdition. Yet his work generally conceals levels of ambiguity beneath the simplistic

tales of hard-working apprentices and foolish rakes — an ambiguity which is analogous to, and frequently relies on, the multi-faceted ingenuity of the artist's manipulation of symbols, forms and meanings.

In this respect, it is significant that a central theme, and recurrent motif, in Hogarth's work is that of choice. On one level, of course, the notion of choice is integral to the anecdotes Hogarth portrays, which invariably deal with the consequences resulting from decisions taken by characters such as the Harlot or Industrious Apprentice about their personal conduct, moral principles and material expectations. (In this sense, too, *Marriage à la mode* is significantly about the expropriation of choice by the fathers of the young couple.) The depiction of choice — good and bad — also enhances the didactic appeal of Hogarth's imagery, since it encourages the viewer to think through their own response to a particular dilemma or decision. Beyond this, however, in highlighting the theme of choice Hogarth was responding to a current aesthetic debate and implictly asserting the superior value of his comic history paintings.

It was the philosopher Anthony Ashley Cooper, Third Earl of Shaftesbury, who had first raised the question in his discussion of history painting, the *Notion of the Historical Draught or Tablature of the Judgement of Hercules* of 1713. Here, Shaftesbury had called for the promotion of sublime history painting and advocated the theme of choice as worthy of the attention of ambitious painters. He illustrated his argument with a story, taken from the *Memorabilia* by the ancient Greek general and writer Xenophon, in which Hercules reaches a crossroads where he is obliged to choose between Virtue and Pleasure (or Vice), personified by two very different female figures. Shaftesbury commissioned a version of the scene from the painter Paulo de Matteis (see page 19), and an engraved illustration of the work by Gribelin adorned the cover of his treatise. The Hercules motif was widely discussed during the eighteenth century and was adapted by such painters as

The Choice of Hercules,
painted by Paolo de Matteis, n.d.
Oil on canvas, 198.2 x 256.5 cm
Ashmolean Museum, Oxford

Sir Joshua Reynolds and Angelica Kauffmann. It is a theme which appears in one of Hogarth's earliest oil paintings, *The Beggar's Opera* (1729, page 47), in which the highwayman Macheath sings 'Which way shall I turn me?' as he is forced to choose between his two 'wives', Polly Peachum and Lucy Lockit. Thereafter, the choice motif — frequently adapted or subverted — recurs in Hogarth's work with almost obsessive frequency.

By insisting so regularly on the theme, Hogarth drew attention to his own claim to be pursuing a form of painting equal in stature to that produced by the sublime history painter. More than this, though, he exploited the classical topos of choice as a means of posing some very awkward questions about the society in which he lived. In the second scene of *An Election* (page 123), for example, an innkeeper plays the role of Hercules confronted not by vice and virtue, but by two crooked political agents, both of whom try to win his vote by slipping him a bribe. Similarly, the grenadier in *The March to Finchley* (page 119) plays an anxious-looking Hercules to the

two women who grasp at his arms, personifying loyalty to the Hanoverian succession and treasonous sympathy for the Catholic Pretender. In some way, too, Tom Rakewell parodies the theme in the first scene of *A Rake's Progress* (page 65), where he stands ineffectually between Sarah Young, the faithful and virtuous girl he now deserts (leaving her pregnant through his own vice), and the pile of money and silver plate, the misuse of which will lead him to further vice and ultimately perdition. Most subversive, perhaps, is Hogarth's use of the theme in the opening scene of *A Harlot's Progress* (see page 20). Here, the innocent country girl is abandoned to the blandishments of Vice (in the shape of the bawd who gently strokes her beneath the chin) by the representative of Virtue, the clergyman seated on horseback, who turns his back on the scene and inspects a letter of introduction to the corrupt Bishop of London, from whom he evidently hopes to receive promotion.

It would seem, then, that choice is all too often tainted or simply wrong, with appropriate consequences. To this extent, Hogarth's modern moral subjects are invariably about the outcome of bad decisions. They pursue the central characters either through an inexorable cycle of degradation provoked by their own folly or portray them as victims of the folly of others. Rather than using painting and engraving to display edifying scenes of virtue, Hogarth presents his heroes and heroines as a dreadful warning of the terrors of transgression and as an admonition against making foolish or short-sighted choices. This negative strategy follows the opinion expressed by Fielding that 'we are much better and easier taught by the examples of what we are to shun, than by those which would instruct us what to pursue.' Indeed, when Hogarth departed from his usual method and sketched out a series celebrating a *Happy Marriage*, he seems to have found the project unappealing and abandoned it at a relatively early stage.

Hogarth's first excursion into the modern moral subject, *A Harlot's Progress*, seems to apply Fielding's

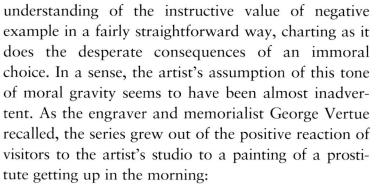

A Harlot's Progress, *1732.*
*Plates 1-4 of a series of six engravings*
*British Museum, London*

understanding of the instructive value of negative example in a fairly straightforward way, charting as it does the desperate consequences of an immoral choice. In a sense, the artist's assumption of this tone of moral gravity seems to have been almost inadvertent. As the engraver and memorialist George Vertue recalled, the series grew out of the positive reaction of visitors to the artist's studio to a painting of a prostitute getting up in the morning:

*This thought pleased many. Some advised him to make another to it as a pair, which he did. Then other thoughts encreas'd and multiplyd by his fruitful invention til he made six different subjects [in] which he painted so naturally the thoughts, and striking the expressions that it drew every body to see them.*[5]

As Ronald Paulson has established, the direction taken by Hogarth in transforming his single episode into a sequential *Progress* was shaped by events recently featured in the London press. As he had demonstrated in *The Beggar's Opera* (page 47), Hogarth was sensitive to the ways in which social eminence could cloud fundamental similarities between the apparently respectable denizens of high life and the more marginal criminal classes. The extent to which there was one law for the rich and

another for the poor became vividly apparent in 1729-30 when a series of scandals and misdeeds proceeded to have very different outcomes according to the social background of the accused. In December 1729 the arrest took place of the notorious highwayman James Dalton (whose wig box Hogarth shows stored on top of the Harlot's bed in plate 3 of the *Progress*). Several weeks later another highwayman, Francis Hackabout, was convicted of robbery at the Old Bailey, while his sister Kate enjoyed a brief notoriety in August 1730 when she was committed to hard labour after being apprehended for keeping a disorderly house by the Westminster magistrate Sir John Gonson. Finally, in April 1731, while Hogarth was hard at work on the *Harlot*, the noted procuress Elizabeth Needham was placed in the pillory in Park Place, where she suffered such severe physical abuse that she died four days later as a result of her injuries.

This litany of low-life dramas was almost overshadowed by the extraordinary events which had surrounded the trial of the wealthy gambler and libertine

Colonel Francis Charteris, who was convicted at the Old Bailey in February 1730 for the rape of his maid servant, Anne Bond. Despite his appalling reputation for sexual misconduct, on 10 April a royal pardon was granted to Charteris, who had connections with the prime minister Sir Robert Walpole. On the same day, James Dalton was sent to the gallows, a fate which befell Francis Hackabout a week later.

Though none of these events is literally mirrored in *A Harlot's Progress*, they undoubtedly shaped the narrative which Hogarth devised around his initial scene. Not only did recent news provide him with significant inspiration in developing his cast of characters, it also lent a degree of complexity to what otherwise might have remained a relatively two-dimensional tale of innocence corrupted. The fate of the harlot Moll Hackabout — the significant name only becoming apparent in scene six, from the inscription on her coffin — cannot be separated from the seamy world of London low life which Hogarth used as his setting. It is this environment which provides the moral foil for the way in which we are to interpret Moll's fate and to understand the choices that lead to her eventual downfall.

The innocent country girl whom we first encounter shortly after her arrival at the Bell Inn in Cheapside is immediately accosted by Mother Needham, who is apparently acting on behalf of Charteris, the thick-set figure who stands in the tavern doorway with his pimp, John Gourlay. The identity of these notorious figures was quickly recognized by Hogarth's contemporaries, who could well understand that Moll would prove easy prey to such hardened libertines — particularly since the representative of the church so conspicuously fails to fulfil his moral duty. Her fall from grace is initially accompanied by a rapid social ascent: in the second plate of the series (see page 20), Moll has become the mistress of a rich Jew, whose attention she tries to distract by kicking over the tea table in order to allow her clandestine lover to make good his escape.

Plate three (see above) shows the price that Moll has been made to pay for her treachery. No longer enjoying the material comforts of the kept woman, she now breakfasts in the dingy room in Covent Garden from which she operates as a prostitute. The fine china and elegant furnishings have been relinquished for cracked bowls and a clumsy stool; instead of an elegant ladies' maid, Moll is now tended by a coarse and ugly servant whose deformed nose bears the ravages of disease. As Moll displays a pocket watch, presumably filched from an unwary

A Harlot's Progress, 1732.
*Plates 5-6 of a series of six engravings*
*British Museum, London*

client, she herself fails to notice the advancing group of bailiffs intent on her arrest. They are led by Sir John Gonson, who had been responsible for apprehending Moll's real-life counterpart, Kate Hackabout in August 1730. Alluding to Gonson's notorious harshness with miscreants, Hogarth decorates Moll's squalid lodgings with a print of Abraham sacrificing Isaac. Though an angel intervenes to stay the patriarch's hand, Moll can expect no such clemency from the unbending magistrate.

Confined to the Bridewell prison, where she is made to beat hemp with the other inmates (see page 21), Moll cuts a pathetic figure as she wields her mallet, still wearing the finery which recalls more prosperous days. Her elegant dress attracts the derision of a hideous old woman, while the glaring warder threatens her with punishment for her feeble efforts. Moll's servant shares her punishment, and sits in the corner leering at her mistress's difficulties. None the less, she remains loyal to the ailing harlot whom we next discover, apparently some years later, on the point of succumbing to the venereal disease contracted from a life of vice (see above). As the miserable woman expires, her small son shows more interest in the food cooking at the open grate. The old woman employed to lay her out rifles through the contents of

the harlot's trunk while two notorious quacks, Doctor Rock and Doctor Misaubin, hotly dispute the merits of their respective cures for syphilis, entirely unconcerned by the fate of their dying patient.

This indifference is echoed in the final scene (see above), where the mourners around Moll's coffin show little grief for the dead woman herself. The old servant uses the casket as a drinks table; the parson spills his brandy as his right hand burrows beneath the skirt of the smiling woman by his side; the undertaker accosts one of the prostitutes, while two others devote their attention to the diseased finger which one displays; the extravagantly gesturing woman on the right is carried away by alchohol rather than emotion. As the harlot's small son, dressed up as chief mourner, happily plays with his spinning top, another mourner removes the coffin lid to gaze on Moll's body as a sort of memento mori. From the inscription on the small metal plaque, we learn that the dead woman was only twenty-three years old.

The *Harlot's Progress* like the *Rake's Progress* and *Marriage à la mode*, is certainly designed as a cautionary tale and as a demonstration of the price to be paid for flouting society's rules. In each instance, however, Hogarth constructs his narrative in such a way as to encourage the viewer to pose broader questions about the circumstances surrounding his characters' fate. Undoubtedly, the harlot stands accused as a common prostitute, the rake as a wastrel and a fraud, while it is the young married couple's faithlessness which precipitates their domestic tragedy. In every instance, however, Hogarth implies that deeper forces are at work, conspiring against the central characters by limiting their freedom of choice, leaving them vulnerable to the fate which befalls them. The harlot is the classic innocent abroad, left unprotected against the advances of the scheming Mother Needham, who snares her into a life of vice. In *A Rake's Progress* Tom Rakewell, too, proves vulnerable to the abuse of riches, but only because his father has so conspicuously failed to use his fortune wisely and fashionable society abounds with predators willing to flatter the inexperienced and immature. Finally, it is the increasing vogue for arranging marital alliances between wealth and birth, to the sole advantage of the older generation, that deprives the young couple of free choice and traps them in a loveless, hopeless marriage.

This sense of moral complexity underpinning the apparently simplistic message of the modern moral subject reaches its peak in what seems at first sight Hogarth's most straightforwardly didactic work — *Industry and Idleness* (see pages 24 and 26). The relatively unsophisticated style of the series, together with the comparatively low asking price of twelve shillings, suggests that Hogarth's intended audience included people similar to the protagonists in his tale. Indeed, the artist emphasized the wholesome moral intent of prints which were:

*calculated for the use and Instruction of youth wherein every thing necessary to be known was to be made as intel-*

*ligible as possible[,] and as fine engraving was not necessary to the main design provided that which is infinitely more material viz that characters and Expressions were well preserved, the purchase of them became within the reach of those for whom they [were] chiefly intended.*

The last point is, of course, debatable. At the equivalent of nearly a month's wages, it is unlikely that too many apprentices invested in the series, though the prints may have appealed to their employers as an appropriately edifying way of brightening up the workshop. The tradition of such moral homilies was well established in the theatre, stretching back to Ben Jonson's collaboration with Marston and Chapman on *Eastward Hoe*, and embracing George Lillo's popular success: *The London Merchant* of 1731. Hogarth seems to borrow certain general themes from both sources, though in essence his tale of the contrasting fortunes of Francis Goodchild and Tom Idle is entirely his own. The opposition between the two men is established in the first print of the series (see page 24), which shows Goodchild working hard at his loom, while Idle is caught dozing by his irate master. The two apprentices' differing attitudes towards their labours is conveyed both through the biblical inscriptions beneath the scene and in the details Hogarth distributes around the workshop. The neatly groomed Goodchild stands before a wall decorated with ballads on Dick Whittington and 'The London Prentice', his copy of 'The Prentice's Guide' lying open in pristine condition by his loom. Tom Idle's negligent appearance is mirrored in his coarse taste in ballads — 'Moll Flanders' — and in the dog-eared 'Prentice's Guide', which lies neglected and torn as a cat plays with his abandoned shuttle and a tankard of ale stands prominently on his loom.

The next eight prints in the series establish a counterpoint between Idle's descent from mischief to criminality and Goodchild's promotion to wealth and domestic bliss. While Idle turns to thieving and consorts with a prostitute who finally betrays him to the authorities, Goodchild marries his employer's daugh-

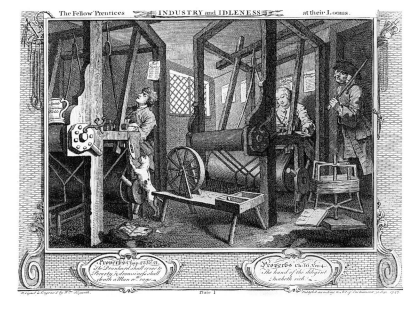

ter, is offered a partnership in the firm and becomes Sheriff of London. The two men's final encounter (see page 26), when Idle is brought before Goodchild in his capacity as magistrate, apparently contrasts desperate remorse with sorrowful compassion. Idle is convicted and taken for execution at Tyburn while Goodchild crowns his glorious ascent by promotion to Lord Mayor of London. Vice and virtue, it seems, have followed directly opposing paths with clearly distinguishable consequences.

Taken at face value, this edifying tale holds out the promise of fame and fortune as the reward for hard work and threatens the idle miscreant with severe retribution. Yet, beneath the surface of this seemingly implacable contrast, forces are at work which disturb the moral symmetry of the apprentices' opposing destinies.[6] Goodchild's ascent (which uncannily echoes Hogarth's own alliance with Sir James Thornhill), for example, seems to owe a great deal to the young man's cultivation of his employer's daughter. Indeed, the historian Sean Shesgreen has pointed out that, rather than his local church of Christ Church, Spitalfields, Goodchild has apparently crossed London to worship at St-Martin-in-the-Fields (see page 24 centre right), where he is able to share a pew with the young Miss West.[7] Striking, too, is the way in which Goodchild is invariably juxtaposed with grotesque figures — whether the wizened pew keeper and singing congregation in church, the porter with his scarred complexion and bulbous nose in the workshop (see page 24 above right), or the deformed and fighting beggars who gather outside his house on the morning after his marriage (see page 24 below right). This reaches a telling climax in the banqueting hall (see page 26 above right), where Goodchild is scarcely visible amongst the ranks of hideous aldermen who pointedly ignore the poor petitioners at the

---

Industry and Idleness, 1747.
*Plates 1-6 of a series of twelve engravings*
*British Museum, London*

entrance as they greedily tuck into their meal. Indeed, his promotion as Sheriff has little bearing on moral excellence — the post depended almost entirely on affluence, as an outlay of £5,000 a year was required by the successful candidate.

That Goodchild's world may not be as pristine and respectable as first appears is given added force in the final encounter between the two men (see page 26 centre right). As the manacled Idle leans forward, energetically pleading for clemency, Goodchild shields his eyes in anguish at the sight of his old workmate. His gesture is that of blind Justice, whose closed eyes traditionally signified her impartiality. Here, though, Goodchild's averted gaze prevents him from noticing his assistant, who takes a false oath from Tom's accomplice, whilst surreptitiously pocketing a bribe. The corruption of 'polite' society, hinted at in the banqueting scene, here degenerates into outright criminality. As Hogarth had suggested as far back as *The Beggar's Opera* (page 47), the dividing line between respectability and the underworld may be less clear cut than is generally acknowledged. The point is driven home in the final two scenes (see page 26), which apparently mark the fulfilment of the two men's contrasting histories. Tom Idle is driven towards the gallows at Tyburn, where he is to be hanged; Francis Goodchild drives past the celebrating mob near St Paul's during the Lord Mayor's procession. In both images, it is the crowd rather than the central characters who are most conspicuous, and in each print they are presented as jostling, shouting, fighting, pushing and falling — an anarchic mass of uncontrolled humanity conspicuous by its similarities rather than its differences.

The world of the apprentice was an onerous one — and the history of Hogarth's relationship with Ellis Gamble suggests his own reservations over the system. As Dorothy George, historian of eighteenth-century London, has pointed out, life was particularly unpleasant in the city's important cloth manufacturing sector:

The IDLE 'PRENTICE return'd from Sea, & in a Garret with a common Prostitute.

The INDUSTRIOUS 'PRENTICE grown rich, & Sheriff of London.

The IDLE 'PRENTICE betray'd by his Whore, & taken in a Night Cellar with his Accomplice.

The INDUSTRIOUS 'PRENTICE Alderman of London, the Idle one brought before him & Impeach'd by his Accomplice.

The IDLE 'PRENTICE Executed at Tyburn.

The INDUSTRIOUS 'PRENTICE Lord-Mayor of London.

*At its best, weaving in Spitalfields was an unhealthy occupation; work at the hand-loom was both sedentary and physically trying; the constant pressing of the bar of the loom against the stomach was a cause of ill health. The work was done in small, crowded rooms in horribly insanitary dwellings, and the air was carefully excluded.*[8]

It is in this light that we must view Tom Idle's rebelliousness, particularly as the fourth plate in the series (see page 24 centre right) suggests that the traditional small workshop in which the two apprentices are initially at work has been superseded by a more intensive production line system in which women and children are also employed. As Shesgreen has pointed out, apprentice weavers were a particularly volatile section of the London labour force, with a record of recurrent violence during the course of the eighteenth century. The publication of instructive manuals, such as the 'Prentice's Guides' featured in plate one, was one of the means by which employers attempted to moralize their workers. On one level, *Industry and Idleness* supplements this propaganda campaign, preaching obedience and hard work to the impressionable apprentice. At the same time, however, Hogarth seems to have secreted a less sententious, more frankly subversive narrative beneath his simple moral tale. It is a message to which the inattentive purchaser may well have remained oblivious, but which none the less paints a bleaker picture, more in keeping with the ambiguities and contradictions of metropolitan existence.

The explicit moral ambition which inspired *Industry and Idleness* encouraged Hogarth to produce such prints in a format more appropriate to an audience of restricted financial means — though, as we have already noted, the price of the series still left it out of reach for ordinary working people. The artist's inter-

Industry and Idleness, 1747.
*Plates 7-12 of a series of twelve engravings*
*British Museum, London*

GIN LANE.

Gin Lane, 1750.
*Engraving, 36 x 30.5 cm*
*British Museum, London*

est in a number of contemporary social issues prompted him to intervene by producing a series of cheap etchings as a means of influencing public opinion. Following the publication in early 1751 of the polemical pamphlet, an *Enquiry into the Cause of the Late Increase in Robbers* by Hogarth's friend, the writer and London magistrate Henry Fielding, he issued two sets of prints tackling the problems of cruelty to animals and public alchoholism, on which Fielding blamed much popular criminality. *The Four Stages of Cruelty* was issued in a vigorous woodcut style at six shillings a set, while he priced *Beer Street*. and *Gin Lane* (1751, see page 35 and above) at one shilling each — still a substantial sum of money when compared to artisans' wages of the period.[9] Hogarth openly referred to his campaigning intent in publicizing his new works, announcing:

*As the Subjects of these Prints are calculated to reform some reigning Vices peculiar to the lower Class of People, in hopes to render them of more extensive use, the Author has publish'd them in the cheapest Manner possible.*

Looking back in his autobiography, Hogarth expressed pride at the beneficial social influence of such initiatives, though others were more sceptical of his motives. Rather than an altruistic contribution to harmony in the workplace, George Vertue dismissed Hogarth's pricing of *Industry and Idleness* merely as a marketing ploy to maximize profits and to match his success with an affluent public with a more popular range of prints. Though such cynicism was probably misplaced, it was in some ways a natural response to Hogarth's extraordinary ingenuity as a commercial operator. From early in his career, he had proved strong-willed, independent and supremely inventive in promoting his works and protecting his financial interest. Hogarth's resentment towards 'the monopoly of printsellers, equally mean, and destructive of the ingenious' encouraged him to eliminate the middle man and publish prints on his own account. His anger at the widespread practice of pirating, which enabled rivals to issue inferior copies of engravings at lower prices, prompted him to agitate for copyright legislation, which Parliament passed in 1735. Thereafter, he skilfully played the market, promoting his prints through subscription, publishing bound volumes of his collected works, initiating novel forms of auction sale and offering original paintings as lottery prizes.

Hogarth was emphatically not working for a mass public; even at his cheapest, his prices compare unfavourably with the rates normally charged for satirical prints, and are substantially higher than those for the woodcuts which were bought by those of modest means. What is, perhaps, most striking about his marketing strategy is his ability to straddle extreme ends of the cultural spectrum, ranging from the chapbook style of *Four Stages of Cruelty* to the polished *Marriage à la mode* (pages 99-109), engraved by specially contracted French craftsmen, from the broad eroticism of *Before* and *After* (pages 55 and 57) to the high seriousness of *Paul before Felix* (page 117). Even as he brazened his common-sense populism and sneered at the inflated reputations of continental masters, Hogarth attempted — perhaps more than any other artist before or since — to excel in both camps, to win fame and fortune as an accessible crowd-pleaser, while commanding respect as a British painter worthy of the great tradition.

Taken at face value, Hogarth comes across as an aggressive vulgarian contemptuous of foreign art and its values, and dismissive of English connoisseurs for their gullible attraction to the 'dark masters' currently flooding the market. His particular *bête noire*, the picture dealer, was blamed for corrupting national taste and depriving native artists of the opportunity to display their talents. Thus, in an essay — significantly published under the pen-name 'Britophil' in June 1737 — he lambasts:

*… picture jobbers from abroad, who are always ready to raise a great cry in the prints whenever they think their craft in danger; and indeed it is in their interest to depreciate every English work as hurtful to their trade of continually importing ship-loads of dead Christs, Holy Families, Madonas [sic], and other dismal dark subjects, neither entertaining nor ornamental, on which they scrawl the terrible cramp names of some Italian masters, and fix upon us poor Englishmen the character of universal dupes.*[10]

Hogarth never tires of illustrating his point, either through the ridiculous foreign paintings he invents to decorate such interiors as the Earl's apartment in *Marriage à la mode* (pages 99-109) or through a satirical squib like *Time Smoking a Picture* (1761, see page 29). His grievance was one commonly voiced by artists trying to make a living in Georgian England —

Time Smoking a Picture, 1761.
*Engraving, 20.3 x 17 cm*
*British Museum, London*

Hogarth's antipathy to foreigners and unshakeable conviction in his own abilities made it inevitable that he would attempt to make a name in the grand manner from which British artists had been so consistently excluded. His means of breaking into the market were ingenious and involved him in a good deal of unpaid labour, which he obviously regarded as a worthwhile long-term investment. Two of his most conspicuous essays in history painting — the staircase decorations for St Bartholomew's Hospital (1736-37, page 81) and *Moses before Pharaoh's Daughter* (1746, page 113) — were the outcome of philanthropic gestures, the latter undertaken as part of an ambitious collective initiative to showcase the talents of British artists at the Foundling Hospital. Though attempts by an essentially comic artist to win recognition as a history painter were mocked as presumptuous by some, Hogarth did succeed in winning several major commissions. No less august a body than the the Honourable Society of Lincoln's Inn was responsible for the artist's purest essay in the grand manner, the *Paul before Felix* (1748, page 117), while in 1755 he was granted a rare opportunity of painting for the Church, when the authorities at St Mary Redcliffe in Bristol offered £525 for an enormous triptych altarpiece. Neither enterprise reveals the artist at his most convincing; however remarkable an achievement it was for a painter and engraver more readily associated with 'low-life' subjects to take on work of such ambition, Hogarth shows himself ill at ease with a pictorial vocabulary in which few English artists of the period had any real experience. *Paul before Felix* advertises its obligation to the Raphael cartoons too openly, and the artist's accomplishment in the field of expression sits rather uncomfortably with the more laconic requirements associated with grand manner history painting.

The humiliation surrounding *Sigismunda* (1759, page 139), Hogarth's most ostentatious — and ultimately misguided — effort in the grand style, ironically reveals how popular success could handicap the artist's bid for recognition as a serious painter. The

in a nation where doctrinal prejudice severely limited church commissions and a combination of parsimony and indifference restricted royal support, British painters were denied opportunities for grand manner painting which their continental counterparts could virtually take for granted. The vogue for picture collecting, which had become a feature of patrician culture, had done little to benefit British artists: as collectors purchased abroad or patronized such foreign visitors as Amigoni, Laguerre or Van Loo, they provided a regular income only to local portraitists, who consequently dominated home production.

genesis of the work in Hogarth's desire to outshine an Italian version of the subject recently auctioned for some £400 is surrounded with hubris. Like some latter-day Marsyas, the painter engaged in an imprudent wager, lost — and was publicly flayed. The time and energy he lavished on the canvas were considerable. As the artist himself ruefully recalled, he 'spent more time and anxiety' on the work 'than would have got me double the money in any of my other way and not half what a common face painter got in the time'. It is, perhaps, this pugnacious sense not only of proving himself against the masters of the past, whom he accused of exerting a posthumous stranglehold over the English market, but also of asserting his superiority over his contemporaries which left Hogarth so vulnerable to critical derision. As his estranged friend John Wilkes remarked on the picture in 1762:

*All his friends remember what tiresome discourses were held by him day after day about the transcendent merit of it, and how the great names of* Raphaël, Vandyke, *&c. were made to yield the palm of beauty, grace, expression, &c. to him, for this long-labour'd, yet still* uninteresting, *single figure. The value he himself set on this, and some other of his works, almost exceeds belief; and from politeness, or fear, or some other motives, he has actually been paid the most astonishing sums, as the price, not of his merit, but of his unbounded vanity.*[11]

Already, Hogarth's efforts at theory in *The Analysis of Beauty* (1753, see above) had attracted much professional disdain. Coming at a time when he seemed an increasingly marginal and cantankerous figure in the English art world, the *Sigismunda* episode made him appear dangerously self-centred and eccentric.

In one crucial respect, Hogarth had already effectively isolated himself from his colleagues by the time of the *Sigismunda* affair. Over a number of years, various initiatives had been attempted to strengthen the corporate identity of English artists in the hope of enhancing their reputation and increasing their market share. Indeed, Hogarth himself had made a

Analysis of Beauty, Plate 1, 1753.
*Engraving, 37.1 x 49 cm*
*British Museum, London*

crucial contribution to this process. In 1735 he had established the St Martin's Lane Academy, which was to serve both as a training school for young artists and as a guild for more established figures. His involvement with the Foundling Hospital, culminating in the display of works donated to the institution in 1747, was an important step in securing a more regular opportunity for exhibiting modern British painting. By the late 1750s, however, Hogarth had become largely estranged from his colleagues' efforts to organize professionally, particularly as regards their efforts to set up a Royal Academy. His objections to such an organization were a mixture of principle and prejudice, largely born from an essentially artisanal notion of what it meant to be an artist. His own commercial, shop-based practice was entirely at odds with the ambitions of younger colleagues such as Reynolds for English artists to be treated as educated practitioners of a liberal profession. It was this artisanal conception which moulded the organization at St Martin's Lane, open to all comers on subscription and run as a democratic institution in which every member's voice was heard. For Hogarth, a formally instituted 'Academy could only compromise this openness, to the detriment of all but a privileged élite:

*I think that this ostentatious establishment can answer no one valuable purpose to the arts, nor be of the least use to any individual, except those who are to be elected professors, and receive salaries, for the kind superintendence they will exercize over such of their bretheren as have not so much interest as themselves.*

Such an institution, Hogarth believed, would only foster bad habits, encouraging students to copy other works of art rather than learning directly from nature, and consolidating the uncritical admiration of old masters which had already so much impeded the progress of painting in England. Worst of all, the sort of institution that supporters of the Academy had in mind was inspired by the most pernicious of models — 'the foolish parade of the French Academy, by the establishment of which Louis XIV got a large portion of fame and flattery on very easy terms'. This was enough to guarantee Hogarth's hostility in its own right. He drove home the point, however, with the claim that what was appropriate for a Catholic nation governed by an absolute monarchy could scarcely work in England, a commercial society in which 'the public encourage trade and mechanics, rather than painting and sculpture.'

In some respects, such views were born from the frustrations that Hogarth himself had encountered in winning recognition as a history painter, rather than from any inherent hostility to the grand manner itself. This, in fact, is one of Hogarth's great paradoxes. On one level, it would be easy to construe his onslaught on the Academy, the connoisseurs and the old masters as a blanket repudiation of tradition in favour of a modernity embodied in the comic history paintings — small-scale works, familiar in theme, accessible in content, and democratic in the reproductive medium through which they were disseminated. Yet, at the same time, it is Hogarth who expended so much energy on history painting at a time when the genre

seemed a lost cause in England; it is Hogarth, too, who peppers his work with references to the art of the past and who, in his responsiveness to such continental fashions as the rococo, might well qualify as one of the most internationally minded British painters of the century.

All of this seems rather hard to credit of the artist who defiantly proclaimed to Mrs Piozzi: 'The connoisseurs and I are at war, you know; and because I hate them, they think I hate Titian, and let them.'[12] Yet it is in such a statement that the solution to Hogarth's relationship with the European tradition is to be found. His truculent provocation reveals less hostility towards the consecrated masters than to their uncritical adulation by self-proclaimed experts, blinded by snobbery and prejudice. And, of course, if his position should be misunderstood by those he so roundly despised; so much the better. It was such an attitude which convinced Hogarth that he could produce a *Sigismunda* to rival anything that the Italian school could produce. As he advises in the caption to *Time Smoking a Picture* (see page 29, issued in 1761 as the subscription ticket for the projected print of *Sigismunda*), 'To Nature and your Self appeal,/Nor learn of others, what to feel.' To the uncorrupted eye, capable of distinguishing authentic value from the spurious patina of age, merit depended on the artist's fidelity to the real world rather than to the abstract criteria touted by the connoisseurs.

Protected by such scepticism, Hogarth confronted the European tradition with a mixture of defiance and respect. Respect there certainly was, as is clear in the way in which he learns from the masters and quotes from their example in the major history pieces. The Venetians at St Bartholemew's Hospital, Poussin in *Moses before Pharaoh's Daughter*, Raphael in *Paul before Felix* and the Bristol altarpiece (pages 81, 113 and 117) — all provide both inspiration and a measure against which the artist feels confident enough to test himself. His familiarity with the art of the past could be put to more subversive use, too, as in *Paul before Felix Burlesqued,* where Hogarth displays his virtuosity in a Rembrandtesque pastiche of his own imitation of Raphael. This playfulness, assuming an ingenuity and lack of pomposity shared with his public, inspired exercises in the 'intricacy' that Hogarth so enjoyed. Most conspicuously, some of the master themes from western art could be taken and turned upside down, often for ironic effect. The harlot's encounter with Mother Needham, for example, recalls the Visitation, her arrest resembles the Annunciation, while the funeral party in the final plate recalls the Last Supper — a motif also conscripted for *The Election Entertainment* (page 121), a decidedly profane occasion! Through such subliminal references, Hogarth was able to multiply the levels of meaning within a single image, persuading the alert spectator that pursuing 'a wanton kind of chace'[13] would be rewarded through added insight and amusement.

Yet beyond this plundering of the 'musée imaginaire' of the past, Hogarth was also exceptionally responsive to contemporary developments in Continental art. From the early conversation pieces on, he reveals a particular interest in French rococo, and was sufficiently impressed by the standard of craftsmanship available in France to cross the Channel in 1743 specifically to engage engravers to work on *Marriage à la mode*. Artists such as Watteau, Lancret, Rigaud and Quentin de la Tour all seem to have had a direct impact on Hogarth's art, while Frederick Antal has argued persuasively for the profound obligation he owes to the seventeenth-century engraver Jacques Callot. Hogarth's peremptory dismissal of French interior decoration as 'all gilt and beshit'[14] conceals a deeper affinity, embodied in the artist's vaunted serpentine Line of Beauty, which his aesthetic writings did so much to promote. Nor do Hogarth's own contacts in the London art world sustain the caricature of the pugnacious British bulldog snapping at the ankles of the affected foreigner. It was a Frenchman — Louis Chéron — with whom he worked at St Martin's Lane in the early 1720s, another Frenchman — Hubert

The Invasion, Plate 1, France, 1756.
*Engraving, 29.2 x 37.8 cm*
*British Museum, London*

Gravelot — from whom he learnt about new developments in rococo during the 1730s, and a further Frenchman — his close friend the enameller Jean-André Rouquet — who did so much to publicize his work on the continent in the 1740s.

Yet the Francophobia which runs through Hogarth's satires and peppers his writings is more than a merely provocative pose. On one level, it was entirely typical of his age. The regular confrontation between the two nations in a succession of wars across the century stoked a widespread dislike which only a small coterie of cosmopolitan aristocrats did not share. Confronted by 'this ambitious, perfidious, restless, bigoted, persecuting, plundering Power', as an anonymous pamphleteer described the country in 1756,[15] Hogarth enthusiastically endorsed perceptions of France as a priest-ridden autocracy pathetically inferior to Protestant England, but constantly presenting a threat to national security. The emaciated guardsmen and bigoted clerics in *Calais Gate* (1748, page 115) fed on a well-developed anti-Gallican iconography which Hogarth taps again in *The Invasion* prints of 1756 (see page 32 opposite). The familiar combination of clownish soldiers, meagre fare and inquisitorial monks provides a pathetic foil to their boisterous British opponents, and the verse caption to the print leaves no doubt over the outcome of any imprudent military adventure: 'Soon we'll teach these bragging Foes,/ That Beef and Beer give heavier Blows,/ Than Soup and Roasted Frogs.'

All of this is entirely predictable. Yet there is another aspect of Hogarth's antipathy towards the French which, though still characteristic of the period, offers us a useful point of entry to the vexed question of the artist's politics. Though the number of specifically political prints issued by the artist is small, his attitude towards contemporary events is all embracing, informing the modern moral subjects every bit as much as polemics such as *The South Sea Scheme* and *The Times* (see pages 37 and 38). A recurrent motif in Hogarth's work, exemplified by the Earl's son in *Marriage à la mode*, is the Frenchified dandy (page 99). Overdressed, self-regarding and effeminate, the dandy was a common butt of Georgian satirists. If French, he was invariably shown as an incongruous mixture of pretension and poverty, his preening affectation jarring absurdly with his emaciated frame and threadbare finery. His British cousin was normally a young aristocrat, like Squanderfield, who had been dazzled by the superficial elegance of the French during the Grand Tour, or a member of the commercial classes, desperate — like Tom Rakewell — for acceptance in the rarefied world of London society. Such figures epitomized what many regarded as a broader corruption of British customs and culture by insidious foreign fashions — particularly from France — which threatened not only the character but also the moral fabric of the nation.

Hogarth's cultural nationalism, evident in his 'war with the connoisseurs', reached back to his very earliest productions as a satirist. In *Masquerades and Operas* (1724, see above), he attacks fashionable

Masquerades and Operas, 1723–4.
*Engraving, 12.7 x 29.7 cm*
*British Museum, London*

enthusiasm for Italian opera and for the masquerades organized by the Swiss promoter Heidegger. The crowds flocking to their doors, are indifferent to the waste-paper merchant carrying off the works of Congreve, Dryden and Shakespeare in a wheelbarrow. British values, Hogarth implies here and elsewhere,[16] are being fast eroded by continental ways, a process which can only be to the nation's detriment. Behind this inexorable demoralization lay the nation's oldest enemy, France. As the novelist Tobias Smollett remarked in his *Travels through France and Italy* of 1766:

*France is the general reservoir from which all the absurdities of false taste, luxury, and extravagance have overflowed the different kingdoms and states of Europe. The springs that fill this reservoir, are no other than vanity and ignorance.*[17]

Resistance to foreign ways went further than a simple preference for native traditions. Rather, cosmopolitanism was opposed in certain quarters as an immediate threat to the moral health and political vitality of the nation. The key word in this debate was 'luxury', a term whose currency in the eighteenth century was matched only by its flexibility of meaning. In essence, luxury referred to the breakdown of ordered social hierarchy through the elevation of private indulgence over public interest. Amongst the wealthy, cultivation of the superficial refinements of fashionable life — fine clothes, extravagant manners, ostentatious buildings and furnishings — was said to encourage a neglect of civic duties and to foster political corruption and military weakness. The lower orders, meanwhile, stood accused of forgetting their rightful place, of becoming insubordinate and slothful, immoral in their lifestyles and presumptuous in imitating the fashions of high society. The inherited strengths of British life, as they were understood at the period, were placed in jeopardy: in the minds of many, liberty, prosperity and international supremacy were threatened by despotism, poverty and vulnerability to foreign attack. By the mid-century, Hogarth's friend Henry Fielding had joined many others in sounding the alarm: 'The fury after licentious and luxurious pleasures is grown to so great a height, that it may be called the characteristic of the present age.'[18]

Fielding's warning is echoed by Hogarth in a variety of ways. His repeated mockery of continental fads, from fine clothes to fine painting, joins the chorus of jeremiads predicting national decline, as native simplicity and plain dealing give way to artifice and effeminacy. Virtue is under pressure at every turn in Hogarth's world: prostitutes try to distract soldiers from their patriotic duty in *The March to Finchley* (1749-50, page 119); fine ladies are pressed into adultery by young suitors in *The Lady's Last Stake* (1758-59, page 137) and *Marriage à la mode*; drunkenness and gambling define the world of the rake; innocence is debauched by the lure of the city in the *Harlot*, and even the apparently blameless Goodchild leaves behind his apprenticeship for the greedy and self-serving world of the London merchant.

As many contemporaries bemoaned the seeming impossibility of distinguishing the true gentleman from the false, the mistress from the serving maid, so Hogarth paints a bleak picture of a society in which individuals attempt to get on in the world by illegitimate short-cuts rather than true merit. Both the harlot and the rake leave their humble origins behind, one using immoral means to get ahead, the other using a fortune he has done nothing to earn to pass himself off as a man of quality. For an age obsessed by the confusion of rank brought about through the growth in commerce and trade, characters such as the harlot and the rake were potent figures. Instructive (and, to some, comforting) though their apparently inevitable come-uppance might have proved, they would have struck a chord in a society where, it was widely believed:

*Money is shifted from hand to hand in such a blind fortuitous manner, that some men shall from nothing in an instant acquire vast estates with the least desert; while others are as suddenly stript of plentiful fortunes.*[19]

The message is hammered home in *Marriage à la mode* (pages 99-109) with its dire warning about the penalties of inter-marriage across the social divide. And while the upper classes ignore their responsibilities in an orgy of self-indulgence and immorality, so the whole fabric of society is placed in jeopardy. The nightmare of *Gin Lane* (1750, see page 27) is not simply one of endemic alchoholism brought about by the uncontrolled sale of cheap liquor. The disorder runs deeper than this; such anarchy is also the outcome of luxury, with the lower orders running riot as their social superiors turn away from their rightful roles as moral guardians. It was Fielding again who had diagnosed the consequences of popular luxury, writing in his *Enquiry into the Cause of the late Increase of Robbers* of:

*the very Dregs of the People, who aspiring still to a Degree beyond that which belongs to them, and not being able by the Fruits of honest Labour to support the State which they*

BEER STREET.

Beer, happy Produce of our Isle
Can sinewy Strength impart,
And wearied with Fatigue and Toil
Can chear each manly Heart.

Labour and Art upheld by Thee
Successfully advance,
We quaff Thy balmy Juice with Glee
And Water leave to France.

Genius of Health, thy grateful Taste
Rivals the Cup of Jove,
And warms each English generous Breast
With Liberty and Love.

*Beer Street, 1750–1.*
*Engraving, 55.9 x 30.3 cm*
*British Museum, London*

———————

*affect, they disdain the Wages to which their Industry would entitle them; and abandoning themselves to Idleness, the more simple and poor spirited betake themselves to a State of Starving and Beggary, while those of more Art and Courage become Thieves, Sharpers and Robbers.*[20]

With Fielding's words in mind, *Beer Street* (see above) provides a revealing glimpse of an ideal society. 'Here', as Hogarth himself remarked, 'all is joyous and thriving. Industry and jollity go hand in hand.' In this well ordered scene, the various classes intermingle in a state of harmony, industry and leisure are properly balanced, prosperity is shared by all but the pawnbroker — who runs the only business to

flourish amidst the squalor of *Gin Lane*. The Englishness of the scene is insistent. The drinkers are solid, straightforward working men — a butcher, a blacksmith and a paviour. In the first state of the print the blacksmith tackles a scrawny French sailor, whom he casually hoists into the air; in a later version of the scene, the foreigner is replaced by that most English of emblems, a shoulder of mutton. To eliminate all ambiguity, the paper lying open on the table at the butcher's side quotes King George II's speech to Parliament of 29 November 1748: 'Let me earnestly recomend [*sic*] to you the Advancement of our Commerce and cultivating the Arts of Peace, in which you may depend on my hearty Concurrence and Encouragement.' Finally, in the verse beneath the print, good old English beer is extolled for its health-giving qualities and its contribution to the nation's superiority.

The bullish nationalism which could conceive *Beer Street* as a model of ordered prosperity founded on the liberties of the free-born Englishman was troubled by a niggling pessimism, however. For Hogarth, as for many others concerned by the direction in which the nation was headed, modern society was tainted by two corrosive diseases which threatened to poison public spirit and sow the seeds of moral and political decline. Both threats — financial speculation and parliamentary corruption — were at one and the same time symptoms and causes of luxury. Both, it was feared, loosened the bonds of duty which had allowed Britons a level of freedom, affluence and power unrivalled in continental Europe by transforming citizens committed to the common good into rapacious and unprincipled egotists. Trade, so critics asserted, 'gives rise to fraud and avarice, and extinguishes virtue and simplicity of manners'.[21] Worse still, speculation on the stock market was thought to encourage profiteering and plundering of national assets by men whose unchecked influence enabled them, in the words of Defoe, 'to declare a new sort of Civil War among us when they please'.[22] Or, as Viscount Bolingbroke, a leading advocate of reform and opponent of Walpole, summed up the situation: 'The power of money as the world is now constituted is real power.'[23]

It was the damaging consequences of this new power in the land which Hogarth attacked in his first satirical print, *The South Sea Scheme* (1721, see page 37). The object of his scorn was the speculative scramble which followed an agreement by the South Sea Company to take on £30 million pounds of the national debt in January 1720. Though the terms of the agreement and the company's commercial interests turned out to be less solid than originally assumed, over the summer trading in South Sea stock reached fever pitch. By September, however, confidence had faltered and the company's value plummeted virtually overnight. Lucky investors escaped at the opportune moment with large profits, yet the majority of speculators faced substantial losses and many were ruined entirely. Revelations that the whole enterprise had been mired in a web of corruption ensnaring both court and government increased the gravity of the scandal.

It is this general sense of the anarchy and moral bankruptcy unleashed by the lure of financial gain that Hogarth explores in his print. The milling crowd of speculators wait for the chunks of flesh which the devil cuts from 'Fortune's golden haunches', while pickpockets profit from the general commotion to filch their purses. The inversion of values is symbolized in the merry-go-round, a wheel of fortune on which a Scots nobleman, a cleric, a prostitute and a hideous hunchback ride together. In the foreground, Honour and Honesty are tortured while Trade languishes from neglect in the shadows. As 'Arts and honest trading drop', so mendacity thrives and national interest is sacrificed to personal gain.

Accusations of political corruption echoed claims that public spirit had been fatally compromised in national life. The Whigs' monopoly of power under the first two Georges, from 1714 to 1760, allowed an elabo-rate system of patronage to be constructed as a means both of bolstering the ministry and of rewarding its supporters. Opponents, particularly those associated with the Tory party, accused Sir Robert Walpole and his successors in power of lining their own pockets and of sacrificing the nation's balanced constitution in the interests of ministerial authority. As the opposition journal *The Craftsman* claimed in 1729, 'Mixt Government' under Walpole had been replaced by a system in which the prime minister had become 'in reality a Sovereign; as despotick, arbitrary a Sovereign as this part of the World affords'.[24] The extension of a system of party loyalties, often founded on direct personal obligation, prompted vocal attacks on the way in which public life had been debased by a factionalism which could only endanger the authentic interests of the nation at large.

As David Dabydeen has shown,[25] Hogarth's work abounds in hidden attacks on Walpole and his cronies. Indeed, following the success of *A Harlot's Progress* (see pages 20-22), the artist was encouraged by ministerial opponents to take on the government directly in a satirical *Statesman's Progress*. He declined the offer, but continued to display his disillusionment with British political life in his work even after Walpole's resignation in 1742. The *Election* series of 1753-54 (pages 121-127) reveals the artist's despair at the damage caused by party-political corruption as a whole, though in the second scene he does single out the Whigs' leader the Duke of Newcastle for his use of bribes to maintain power. *An Election* is, however, a more comprehensive indictment of political corruption, revealing the cancer of luxury and self-interest sapping the nation's strength nation's. The loss of Minorca to the French in 1756, at the start of the Seven Years' War, gave added edge to Hogarth's attack by the time he had issued the works as engravings in 1758. In *Canvassing for Votes* (page 123), he reminds his viewers of Britain's recent naval supremacy at the battle of Portobello (the name of the pub on the right), where in 1739 Admiral Vernon had captured a Spanish fortress in Panama

See here y Causes why in London, —
So many Men are made & undone,
That Arts & honest Trading drop
To "Swarn about y Devils Shop(A)
Who Cuts out (B) Fortunes Golden Haunches

Trapping their Souls with Lotts & Chances
Shareing out from Blue Garters down
To all Blue Aprons in the Town.
Here all Religions flock together,—
Like Tame & Wild Fowl of a Feather,

Leaving their strife Religious bustle,
Kneel down to play at pitch & Hussle(C)
Thus when the Sheepherds are at play;
Their flocks must surely go Astray;
The woeful Cause y in these Times,—

(D) Honour, & honesty, are Crimes,—
That publickly are punish'd by
(G) Self Interest and (F) Vilany;—
So much for Mony's, magick power
Guess at the Rest, you find out more.
price 1 Shilling

*South Sea Scheme, 1721.*
*Engraving, 22.2 x 31.7 cm*
*British Museum, London*

against all the odds. His conviction that such glory had been forfeited by internal corruption was driven home in an engraved version of the print in which the lion figurehead devouring a fleur-de-lis has no teeth.

Hogarth, it seems, shared a common view that the nation had been hijacked by the politicians. Indeed, this belief is given emblematic force in *The Polling* (page 125), where we see Britannia stranded in her carriage, ignored by the footmen who carry on their

card game, unaware that the coach is on the point of collapse. The need to rescue the reins of power from such irresponsible hands and to set the carriage of state on the high road of freedom and public interest once more had become a priority for those who

Designed & Engraved by W Hogarth

*The Times*
Plate I

Published as the Act Directs
Sep.r 7.ᵗʰ 1762

The Times, Plate 1, 1762.
*Engraving, 21.7 x 29.5 cm*
*British Museum, London*

feared that calamity would result from the Whigs' continuing monopoly of power. Opposition to the government had crystallized in the 1740s over the estranged son of George II, Frederick, Prince of Wales, whose circle at Leicester House dreamt of a new age of virtue in which monarch and government would work together for the common good. A new political programme was elaborated by the Tory thinker Henry St John, Viscount Bolingbroke, who convinced Frederick of the need for a 'Patriot King' to sweep away faction and corruption. Such a monarch would rule the nation not as the hostage of a particular party, but as the guide of a ministry formed of men of good will, unencumbered by factional ties. Instead of a 'king without monarchical splendour, a senate of nobles without aristocratical independency, and a senate of commons without democratical freedom',[26] balance would be restored to government and the kingdom would flourish.

Frederick's death in 1751 seemed to put such a project in jeopardy, but the accession of his son George III in 1760 suggested that the Whigs' days were numbered. George had inherited many of his father's ideas through the influence of his tutor, the Scots nobleman Lord Bute. The new king's determination to break the Whigs, end corruption and reassert regal power over a ministry of 'patriots' was stiffened by his commitment to bring to an end the war with France which had raged since 1756. The resignation in 1761 of the hugely popular Whig politician William Pitt, who was committed to pursuing the war as a means of consolidating Britain's colonial supremacy, allowed George to make his move. Promoting Bute to head the ministry, he authorized peace negotiations which in 1762 led to the Treaty of Paris, the terms of which were widely criticized for failing to capitalize on Britain's military superiority.

Bute fast became the target of a virulent campaign of satirical prints in which he was accused of adultery with the king's mother, corruption, despotic ambitions and every imaginable personal vice. In the midst of this storm of abuse, Hogarth published one of his last — and certainly most controversial — prints: *The Times. Plate 1* (1762, see page 38). Of several hundred satires published on Lord Bute, Hogarth's is one of a small handful to support the new ministry and its search for peace. In one of his most complex emblematic designs, Hogarth portrays Bute as a fireman, attempting to damp down the flames which consume the globe on a building which symbolizes the international dimensions of the war. While his Scots supporters bring buckets of water to his engine, ministerial opponents attempt to frustrate their efforts. In the foreground, one of Pitt's supporters attempts to trip them with his wheelbarrow full of copies of the opposition papers, the *Monitor* and *North Briton*. In a building identified as the 'Temple Coffee House', Pitt's brother-in-law, Earl Temple,

tries to dislodge Bute with a jet of water. His efforts are backed up by the opposition journalists John Wilkes and Charles Churchill, who lean from attic windows and fire liquid on Bute from clyster pipes. In the street below, Pitt himself (disguised as Henry VIII in some versions of the print) stands on stilts and blows his bellows to fan the flames which Bute is trying to extinguish. The millstone around his neck recalls the £3,000 pension he had accepted on his resignation, though this lapse in his much-vaunted integrity does not seem to have antagonized the merchants and aldermen who offer their encouragement.

This vigorous gesture in support of a much-hated minister unleashed a torrent of abuse on the ailing artist. Hogarth himself became an object of public ridicule in the satirical prints, which accused him of selling his soul to the government (he had been appointed to the largely honorary post of Serjeant Painter to the King by George II in 1757), derided the pretensions of his *Analysis of Beauty* and mocked the public humiliation of the *Sigismunda* débâcle. Stung by Hogarth's attack on his Pittite stance, John Wilkes published a violent denunciation of the artist in the *North Briton,* in which he accused his former friend of malice and claimed that his ill-judged essay in political satire confirmed the decline in his talents:

*I own that I am grieved to see the genius of* Hogarth, *which should take in all ages and countries, sunk to a level with the miserable tribe of etchers, and now, in his rapid decline, entering into the poor politics of the faction of the day, and descending to low personal abuse, instead of instructing the world, as he could once do, by manly moral satire. Whence can proceed so surprising a change? Is it the forwardness of old age which is come upon him? or is it that envy and impatience of resplendent merit in every way at which he has always sickened?*[27]

Wilkes soon got his come-uppance, as we have seen. So too did his associate, Charles Churchill, contemptuously dismissed by Hogarth as 'Wilkes's toadeater'. In June 1763 he published his crude and cruel

*Epistle to William Hogarth*. Again, it is the artist's inflated view of his talents, his jealousy at the success of others and his inability to recognize his limitations as a comic painter which Churchill exploits in his attack. Though he concedes that Hogarth's genius transcends his personal failings, his onslaught ends with a sneering question to the ageing painter:

*Thou* wretched Being, *whom, on Reason's plan,*
*So chang'd, so lost, I cannot call a Man,*
*What could persuade Thee, at this time of life,*
*To launch afresh into the Sea of Strife?*
*Better for Thee, scarce crawling on the earth,*
*Almost as much a child as at thy birth,*
*To have resign'd in peace thy parting breath,*
*And sunk unnotic'd in the arms of Death.*[28]

However distastefully put, Churchill's question is a challenging one. Now aged sixty-six and in poor health, Hogarth must have recognized that support for a figure as unpopular as Bute from such a celebrated pen could only stir up controversy. Though he claims in his autobiography that, following the frustrations of *Sigismunda*, *The Times* was simply a means 'to recover my lost time, and stop a gap in my income', it is hard to believe that the print was not intended as a gesture of support to a ministry which Hogarth genuinely believed to be capable of saving the nation from political corruption and moral decline. Bute's much-vaunted challenge to the Whigs, his pledge to govern with a broadly based coalition rather than a faction of self-serving hacks, seems to have struck a chord in the old artist. A persistent critic of parliamentary double-dealing under the first two Georges, Hogarth may well have looked to the new reign as a fresh opportunity for the nation under the protection of a 'patriot king'.

Hogarth's optimism seems to have been short-lived. A sequel to *The Times* is more circumspect in its assessment of the political situation, and suggests that Hogarth had come to believe that the change of ministry merely opened the way for a new wave of pen-

sioners and placemen. Its weary cynicism is characteristic of the artist's last years. Frustrated at *Sigismunda*'s reception, increasingly isolated within the artistic community, and now the butt of violent political attacks, Hogarth spent his final months sketching an autobiographical apologia and revising some of his engravings. In April 1764, increasingly plagued by ill health, he published his final print, *Tailpiece: The Bathos* (see page 41). Officially advertised as a decorative coda for the bound volume of his collected engravings, this nihilistic scene represents the end of all things in an exhausted jumble of dejection and decay. Father Time expires, his broken scythe at his side. Around him, in an array of literal and metaphorical visual puns on the theme of gallows humour, the world comes to an end. Nature is bankrupt, the ruler's crown is in fragments, the artist's cracked palette lies abandoned next to a crumpled copy of *The Times*, which begins to smoulder as a candle end ignites its lower edge.

Though his dedication of *The Bathos* 'to the Dealers in Dark Pictures' hints that the familiar combativeness had not been quite extinguished, it is clear that the despondency which soured Hogarth's later years weighed increasingly heavily. His incursion into political controversy had obviously dealt a severe blow to his normally buoyant self-assurance. As he confides in his autobiographical notes, 'My phylosphical friends bid me laugh at the Abusive nonsense of party writers But I cannot rest myself.' Yet the years of laughter and pugnacious self-confidence seemed now to have past and on 25 October 1764, in the home at Leicester Fields to which he had moved at the height of his career in 1742, Hogarth died alone in the night.

## NOTES
[1] All of Hogarth's autobiographical writings are quoted from the 'Anecdotes of William Hogarth, written by himself' in J.B. Nichols, *Anecdotes of William Hogarth*, (London, 1833; reprinted, London, 1970). Though Burke's edition of the notes is considerably more reliable for scholarly purposes, this early transcript, despite its occasional embroidery of the original, has the advantage of clarity over the fragmentary state and often

Tailpiece, or The Bathos, 1764.
*Engraving, 26 x 32.5 cm*
*British Museum, London*

---

obscure phraseology of the artist's manuscript draft.

[2] C. Lamb, 'Essay on the Genius and Character of Hogarth' (1811), reprinted in J.B. Nichols, *Anecdotes of William Hogarth*, p. 92.

[3] Quoted in R. Paulson, *Hogarth. His Life, Art, and Times* (New Haven, 1974), pp. 202-203.

[4] W. Hogarth, *The Analysis of Beauty* (ed. J. Burke), (Oxford, 1955), pp. 41-42.

[5] Quoted in R. Paulson, *Hogarth*, p. 105.

[6] For a detailed analysis of *Industry and Idleness*, see R. Paulson, *Emblem and Expression. Meaning in English Art of the Eighteenth Century* (London, 1975), pp. 58-78.

[7] S. Shesgreen, 'Hogarth's Industry and Idleness: A Reading,' *Eighteenth-century Studies*, vol. 9, 1976, p. 587.

[8] M. Dorothy George, London Life in the Eighteenth Century (Harmondsworth, 1966), p. 194.

[9] "Before 1765, speaking very broadly, labourers' wages varied from 9s. to 12s. a week, 10s. being perhaps the usual rate. The "common wages of a journeyman" in the less well paid trades were then from 12s. to 14s. or 15s.' M.D. George, *London Life*, p. 166.

[10] First published in the *St James's Evening Post*, 7 June 1737, and reprinted in J.B. Nichols, *Anecdotes of William Hogarth* (London, 1833; reprinted, London, 1970), p. 40.

[11] *The North Briton*, no. 17, 25 September 1762, p. 98. The essay is reprinted in full in A. Hamilton, *The Infamous Essay on Woman, or John Wilkes seated between Vice and Virtue* (London, 1972), pp. 57-62.

[12] Quoted in F. Antal, *Hogarth and His Place in European Art* (London, 1962), p. 140.

[13] W. Hogarth, *The Analysis of Beauty*, p. 42.

[14] Quoted in R. Paulson, *Hogarth*, p. 257.

[15] *The Progress of the French, in their Views of Universal Monarchy*, quoted in G. Newman, *The Rise of English Nationalism. A Cultural History 1740-1830* (London, 1987), p. 76.

[16] See, for example, the comic painting *Taste in High Life* of 1742, commissioned by Mary Edwards, in which a ridiculously foppish couple greet each other, while a woman in an extravagant hoop skirt pets a black servant boy in a turban and an elegantly dressed monkey looks on.

[17] T. Smollett, *Travels through France and Italy* (1766; reprinted, London, 1969), pp. 68-69.

[18] H. Fielding, *A Charge delivered to the Grand Jury ... of Westminster* (1749), quoted in J. Sekora, *Luxury. The Concept in Western Thought, Eden to Smollett* (Baltimore, 1977), pp. 89-90.

[19] Anonymous, *An Essay towards preventing the Ruin of Great Britain* (1721), p. 5, quoted in J. Sekora, *Luxury*, p. 82.

[20] J. Fielding, *Enquiry into the Cause of the Late Increase of Robbers* (1751), p. 5, quoted in Sekora, *Luxury*, p. 91.

[21] C. Davenant, *Essay upon the Probable Methods of Making a People Gainers in the Balance of Trade* (1699) vol. 2, p. 275, quoted in Sekora, *Luxury*, p. 79.

[22] D. Defoe, *The Villany of Stock-Jobbers Detected* (1701), quoted in D. Dabydeen, *Hogarth, Walpole and Commercial Britain* (London, 1987), p. 17.

[23] Henry St John, 1st Viscount Bolingbroke, *Dissertation upon Parties* (1733-35), quoted in Sekora, *Luxury*, p. 68.

[24] Quoted in V. Carretta, *The Snarling Muse. Verbal and Visual Political Satire from Pope to Churchill* (Philadelphia, 1983), p. 157.

[25] D. Dabydeen, *Hogarth, Walpole and Commercial Britain* (London, 1987).

[26] Henry St John, 1st Viscount Bolingbroke, *Letters on the Study and Use of History* (1752), quoted in V. Carretta, *The Snarling Muse*, p. 176.

[27] *The North Briton*, no. 17, 25 September 1762, p. 99, from A. Hamilton, *The Infamous Essay on Woman*, p. 59.

[28] C. Churchill, 'Epistle to William Hogarth', in D. Grant (ed.), *The Poetical Works of Charles Churchill* (Oxford, 1956), pp. 211-30. This extract from p. 229.

1697 ❧ 1764

*W<sup>m</sup> Hogarth*

# THE PLATES

One of Hogarth's earliest recorded oil paintings, this satirical scene relates thematically to the contemporaneous *Orator Henley Christening a Child*. Just as that work features the highly unorthodox preacher John Henley, a noted personality in Hanoverian London, so here Hogarth incorporates a likeness of the notorious magistrate Thomas de Veil — a figure who reappears in *Night* from the *Four Times of Day*.

To the obvious amusement of the two fashionable observers on the left, a young woman in an advanced state of pregnancy identifies the father of her child on oath before the magistrate. The old man in a muffler throws his hands up in despair at her accusation while his wife vents her fury, and the true culprit, a handsome youth, prompts the young woman's false testimony. Oblivious to this miscarriage of justice, the magistate looks on pompously, while the child at his side parodies the action by teaching a spaniel to sit up and beg.

Though it displays a rather rudimentary grasp of expression, a field in which Hogarth would later excel, *The Denunciation* contains in embryo many of the elements which would be developed in the modern moral subjects. Confronted by a single image, the spectator is here invited to elaborate the narrative by speculating on events preceding the episode portrayed, and imagining the consequences of the young woman's actions. It seems probable that it was from a similar starting point that the artist evolved the series of tableaux which made up the *Harlot's Progress*, a work which, according to Vertue, grew out of a single scene representing a prostitute's morning levée. As in this and subsequent series, Hogarth here incorporates identifiable personalities and subsidiary groups which comment on the central action. This somewhat wooden scene thus paves the way to Hogarth's most significant contribution to English narrative painting.

# The Denunciation, or A Woman Swearing a Child to a Grave Citizen

*Painted c. 1729*
*49.53 x 66.04 cm*
*National Gallery of Ireland, Dublin*

One of five versions of this scene from John Gay's phenomenally successful work, first performed at Lincoln's Inn Fields in January 1728, *The Beggar's Opera* provided Hogarth with the foundations upon which later modern moral subjects would be developed. The artist selected a climactic moment in the drama, set in Newgate Prison, as the highwayman Macheath, a parodic contemporary Hercules bound and manacled, tries to choose between his two 'wives', Polly Peachum and Lucy Lockit, while both beseech their fathers to have their lover released.

In the same way that Gay's ballad opera questioned the distinction between polite society and the underworld in this satirical attack on Walpole's government, so Hogarth draws an implicit parallel between the fictional world of the stage and the real world embodied in the audience. Framed by the proscenium curtain, with its arms and inscription '*Velute in speculum*' ('Even as in a mirror'), players and public interact in a way which sets up complex resonances that question the distinctions between the two. Most strikingly, Lavinia Fenton, the actress playing Polly, gazes beyond her fictional father to her real-life lover, the Duke of Bolton, who is prominently seated in the audience on the right.

Hogarth's passion for the theatre, and the recurrence of dramatic themes in his work, was typical of an age which witnessed a flowering of portrayals of the stage and of its leading figures, both in England and abroad. More fundamentally, his attitude towards narrative scenes was overtly theatrical in conception, particularly as regards the characterization of the protagonists in his modern moral subjects.

Completed at an early stage in Hogarth's career as a painter, *The Beggar's Opera* provided him with valuable patronage from the impresario John Rich, later a close personal friend, and the M.P. Sir Archibald Grant.

## The Beggar's Opera 5

*Painted 1729*
*59 x 76.2 cm*
*Yale Center for British Art*

The marriage ceremony of Stephen Beckingham, a barrister from a landed family in Kent, to Mary Cox, the daughter of a Kidderminster attorney-at-law, took place in St Benet's church, St Paul's Wharf on 9 June 1729. Hogarth shows the parson reading from the service book and the groom taking his bride's right hand in readiness to place the ring on her finger. Above the couple, two putti borne upon a cloud up-end a cornucopia containing fruit and flowers to celebrate the couple's future prosperity.

An early example of Hogarth's work in oil, this attractive formal group betrays a certain uneasiness with an unfamiliar medium. Stylistic details suggest that the artist may well have called upon the assistance of an architectural painter to provide the setting, which curiously resembles St Martin-in-the-Fields rather than St Benet's itself. While the putti seem to have been painted on top of the completed interior, the artist was obliged to paint out a figure in the left foreground, shown in the original composition kneeling down to arrange the hassocks. The absence of the figure has been compensated for by the brightly coloured carpet in the foreground, which again was apparently added at a late stage.

The identity of the other participants is a matter for conjecture, though the figure in black observing the couple may be the bride's father Joseph Cox, while it has been suggested that the woman in blue at his side may be her late mother.

In its presentation of a fashionable group in an elaborate interior, this work represents one of Hogarth's earliest essays in the conversation piece, a speciality of the painter in the early 1730s, when the genre first came to prominence in English art.

# The Wedding of
# Stephen Beckingham and Mary Cox

*Painted 1729-30*
*128.3 x 102.9 cm*
*The Metropolitan Museum of Art, New York*

In what is perhaps the most Watteau-esque of his conversation pieces, Hogarth portrays the celebrated connoisseur Sir Andrew Fountaine, of Narford Hall, Norfolk, inspecting a mythological landscape painting, apparently oblivious to the beauties of the parkland scene surrounding him. This conceit on the contrast between nature and artifice is further developed in the opposition between the male and female groups, respectively associated with culture and nature, and in the visual pun of the fountain portrayed in the canvas which the auctioneer Cock displays for Sir Andrew's delectation.

Hogarth's painting dates from the end of Fountaine's illustrious and varied public career, which had begun at William III's court in 1696, shortly after his graduation from Oxford. Knighted in 1699, Fountaine had then accompanied Lord Macclesfield to Hanover, carrying the Act of Succession to the Elector in 1701. Over the next two years he travelled Europe, befriending the German philosopher Leibnitz, gaining the confidence of the Elector and Electress Sophia of Hanover, and beginning what was to become a prodigious collection of paintings, drawings and *objets d'art*. Following a second Grand Tour, undertaken between 1714 and 1716, Fountaine was appointed to a number of influential posts at court, culminating in his employment as tutor to George II's third son Prince William Augustus, with whose mother, Queen Caroline, he was closely associated. His final years were spent amidst his collection at Narford, where he had retired in 1732.

Said by the painter Jonathan Richardson the Younger to have 'out-Italianized the Italians themselves', Fountaine was a notably discerning and fashionable client for Hogarth to have won, and it is striking that in *The Fountaine Family* he has produced one of his most elegant and cosmopolitan conversation pieces.

## The Fountaine Family

*Painted c. 1730*
*47.6 x 58.4 cm*
*Philadelphia Museum of Art*

A conversation piece that contained no fewer than twenty-five individual portraits in the miniature, the *Assembly* was commissioned by the Irish peer Viscount Castlemaine to commemorate the twenty-fifth wedding anniversary which he and his wife had celebrated in their sumptuous Palladian mansion at Wanstead in Essex. A member of the wealthy Child banking family, Castlemaine had employed the architects Colen Campbell and William Kent to build and decorate his country seat, and it is in the ballroom designed by Kent that Hogarth depicts the Viscount (seated on the extreme right), his wife (seated at the centre) and their guests. It has been suggested that the artist's antipathy towards Kent led him to exaggerate the highly elaborate furnishings and ornate decoration to the point of parody.

Though their impact is rather overwhelmed by the mêlée, Hogarth infiltrates the composition with a number of emblematic allusions to the subject of marriage. Lady Castlemaine displays an ace of spades — the winning card — to her husband, while between the couple a pair of whippets, signifying fidelity, gaze adoringly at each other (a direct contrast with the later use of two dogs manacled together to signify marital discontent in scene one of *Marriage à la mode*, page 99). As with the modern moral subjects, the paintings on the wall serve as a commentary on the principal action, echoing the theme of marital devotion. Their subjects, Portia and Julia, are both celebrated classical wives who sacrificed themselves for their husbands Brutus and Pompey.

Involving the artist in the doubtless complex and protracted business of arranging sittings with the large number of guests portrayed in the group, the *Assembly at Wanstead House* proved a major undertaking; Hogarth was still at work some two years after Castlemaine's initial commission in August 1729.

# An Assembly at Wanstead House

*Painted 1730-31*
*76.2 x 64.7 cm*
*Philadelphia Museum of Art*

Hogarth painted two versions of the erotic couplet *Before* and *After* (page 57) — in the early 1730s. A woodland setting was used for the earlier treatment, which focuses exclusively on the physical encounter between an ingratiating young beau and an initially reluctant maid. Abandoning the rural backdrop upon returning to the subject, Hogarth introduced suggestive details which allude to the crucial missing link — the carnal encounter itself — in a way which prepares the ground for the use of emblem in *A Harlot's Progress* (see pages 20-22). This was extended in the engravings of *Before* and *After* (1736), in which the artist exploited the greater clarity of the graphic medium to incorporate details absent in the original canvases.

Hogarth's foray into erotic imagery — for which there was considerable demand throughout the century — grew out of a commission for the outdoor scenes from John Thomson, M.P. for Great Marlow. The artist was left with the works on his hands, however, when his patron fled the country having been caught embezzling the profits of the Charitable Corporation for the Relief of the Industrious Poor. The later pair were, according to a contemporary source, ordered by 'a certain vicious nobleman', thought to have been the Duke of Montagu.

In *Before* Hogarth shows a libertine energetically dragging a young woman over to the bed on which he is perched. The girl apparently resists with some force, thrusting her hand against her assailant's forehead and grasping at a dressing table to steady her from collapsing into his embrace. As the table falls, however, we see that its contents — erotic poems by the Earl of Rochester, a volume marked 'Novels' (a literary form widely frowned upon as a source of moral perdition), and 'The Practice of Piety' — suggest an ambivalence which may undermine the vigour of the maid's resistance.

## Before

*Painted c. 1731*
*39.5 x 33.5 cm*
*Collection of the J. Paul Getty Museum, Malibu*

In a scene of post-coital confusion, the libertine pulls on his breeches while his conquest, dishevelled and apparently exhausted, leans against him for support. The small dog, whose friskiness in *Before* mirrored the energetic struggle, now lies dozing next to the fallen dressing table with its broken mirror.

In the engraved version of these scenes, which differ from the paintings in several significant respects, Hogarth added a piquant commentary on the action in the form of the pictures decorating the room — a technique exploited to the full in the modern moral subjects. Instead of the flower piece visible in the original canvases, in plate one Hogarth shows a Cupid igniting a rocket, which takes off in a shower of sparks. In scene two the fallen dresser reveals its companion piece, in which a broadly grinning Cupid watches the spent projectile fall back to earth.

*Before* and *After* represent Hogarth's narrative technique in its basic form. Action is followed by consequence in a linear sequence; the viewer is left to fill in the intervening moments — though cultural convention and ample visual clues mean that there is little ambiguity over what has occurred.

# After

*Painted c. 1731*
*39.5 x 33.5 cm*
*Collection of the J. Paul Getty Collection, Malibu*

Commissioned by George Cholmondeley, Viscount Malpas (later third Earl of Cholmondeley), this curious conversation piece is at once stiffly solemn and profoundly subversive.

Cholmondeley, shown wearing the Order of the Bath, is seated in front of his brother James, a colonel in the 34th Regiment of Foot, and gazes affectionately towards his wife Mary and their youngest son Frederick. The daughter of Sir Robert Walpole, Mary had died of consumption in France the previous year and her body had been lost in a shipwreck whilst being returned home in April 1732. The commemorative function of the family group, together with the need for Hogarth to rely on portraits for his posthumous likeness of Mary, explain the stiffness of her pose and the presence of the putti hovering above her head. The family arms, positioned over Lord Malpas, add to the impression of *gravitas* which suffuses the left-hand side of the image.

The contrast with events on the other side of the room could scarcely be more vivid. Here, the two eldest Cholmondeley boys, George and Robert, engage in their mischief apparently oblivious to the niceties of group portraiture. As George rushes forward, Robert vigorously kicks a pile of books from a low table. The viewer, aware of these antics in a way that the other sitters appear not to be, anticipates the books' fall and the disruption it will cause. In such a way, the solemnity of the image is punctured and a finally optimistic sense of the continuity of life, embodied in the unselfconscious innocence of the children, tempers the restrained, commemorative tone of this remarkable work.

In 1734, Hogarth again portrayed Cholmondeley, in a collaborative project with the sporting artist John Wooton, in which he was paid five guineas a head to paint in the features of various figures, including Frederick, Prince of Wales.

# The Cholmondeley Family

*Painted 1732*
*71.1 x 90.8 cm*
*Private Collection*

This charming scene of amateur theatricals records a performance of Dryden's *The Indian Emperor* at the home of John Conduitt, Master of the Mint, in St George's Street, Hanover Square. In commissioning the scene, Conduitt chose not only to record an important moment in the life of his only daughter Catherine, shown here in black to the right of the stage, but also to commemorate the particularly glittering social occasion which had accompanied the children's performance. While the host and hostess appear only as portraits on the wall above their guests, Hogarth cleverly balances his composition to display the distinguished audience without detracting from the impact of the scene on stage. Here, Catherine and her friends act out a dramatic moment, reminiscent of *The Beggar's Opera* (page 47), in which the Spanish leader Cortez must choose between the love of two Indian princesses.

Amongst the guests, Hogarth draws particular attention to the three royal children, William, Duke of Cumberland, and his sisters Mary and Louisa, who stand before the fireplace immediately behind their governess, Mary, Lady Deloraine. She in turn bends forward, encouraging one of her own daughters to pick up a fallen fan. To her left, the Duchess of Richmond watches the play, while her husband leans on the back of her chair. Behind him, the Earl of Pomfret, wearing the red sash of the Order of the Bath, engages in conversation with Thomas Hill, Secretary to the Board of Trade, while the Duke of Montagu looks on.

The scene is to some extent dominated by a bust of Isaac Newton by Roubiliac over the fireplace. Conduitt, who had succeeded Newton at the Mint and had married his niece Catherine, was the first biographer of his former colleague and friend, whose memory he did much to promote.

# A Scene from 'The Conquest of Mexico'

*Painted 1732-35*
*130.8 x 146.6 cm*
*Private Collection*

This unused preliminary sketch for *A Rake's Progress* offers an interesting insight into Hogarth's compositional technique. In its overall disposition, it resembles *The Rake's Levée* (page 67), particularly as regards the architectural setting, the presence of the waiting figures in the ante-room on the left, and the kneeling jockey in the foreground. Thematically, the scene relates most closely to *The Rake Marrying an Old Woman* (page 73), though at this stage Hogarth apparently intended to advance their union, possibly placing it immediately after the rake's inheritance, to contrast all the more vividly with his abandonment of the pregnant Sarah Young in the opening scene. In the event, he reorganized the narrative whilst retaining elements of the pictorial structure.

Yet, beyond this, Hogarth seems to have exploited the abandoned sketch when composing the opening scene of *Marriage à la mode* (page 99). Not only do both episodes centre on a marriage contract, but in each instance the artist also shows the prospective groom distracted from the business at hand: here, the rake apparently slips a *billet doux* to his servant, while in the later work the Earl's son is more preoccupied by his own reflection than by his fiancée or the negotiations between his father and prospective father-in-law.

The present work, with its conspicuous display of old masters and somewhat battered classical busts, emphasizes the rake's pretensions as a connoisseur. Heads of Cicero, Julia and Germanicus, paragons of virtue, seem to cringe at the transaction they are witnessing, while behind them Jupiter ravishes Ganymede in a work later re-used in the fourth episode of *Marriage à la mode* (page 105). Immediately behind the rake, Hogarth vents his anti-Catholic prejudices with a portrayal of a transubstantiation machine, with the Virgin tossing Holy Infants into the top and a cleric collecting communion wafers at the other end.

# The Marriage Contract

*Painted c. 1733*
*62.23 x 75.56 cm*
*Ashmolean Museum, Oxford*

Hogarth began work on his second moral series within a year of the successful publication of *A Harlot's Progress*, and now turned to the complementary tale of a young rake who squanders his inheritance on high living, only to meet a tragic end in the madhouse at Bedlam. The paintings for the sequence were purchased by William Beckford of Fonthill at the artist's sale in February 1745.

The opening scene introduces us to Tom Rakewell, a young bourgeois who has recently inherited the fortune accumulated by his miserly father, seen poring over his gold in the portrait above the fireplace. Evidence of the old man's obsessive frugality abounds: money comes tumbling from its hiding place in the ceiling, disturbed by the workman hanging mourning drapes; old clothes are hoarded in a cupboard on the left; bills, bonds and indentures lie in a pile next to a strongbox stacked with plate. His foolish son has already set out on a spending spree, and is being measured for a new set of clothes while a steward surreptitiously pockets coins from a table behind his back.

Yet Tom has other responsibilities to face: his former fiancée, Sarah Young, stands weeping as she holds the ring with which Tom once promised her marriage, and her irate mother gestures vigorously to indicate the young woman's advanced state of pregnancy. In response, Tom stares vacantly at the girl, and proffers a handful of money to extricate himself from the situation.

With this opening scene, Hogarth damns both generations of the Rakewell family for their irresponsibility, echoing the common contemporary belief that miserly parents bred spendthrift offspring.

## A Rake's Progress: 1. The Rake Taking Possession of his Estate

*Painted 1733-34*
*62.23 x 74.93 cm*
*Sir John Soane's Museum, London*

An archetypal 'bourgeois gentleman', Tom has moved to fashionable surroundings and has used his money to become a dashing man about town. Still in his nightcap, the young rake is besieged by a troupe of hangers-on. He hopes to acquire from them a veneer of gentility, but they are united only in their desire to part the young wastrel from his newly acquired fortune.

Several of Tom's attendants are recognizable contemporaries. The figure at the harpsichord has been identified as the composer George Frederick Handel; at his side may be the fencing master Dubois, who is surveyed with less than enthusiasm by a quarter-staff player, traditionally thought to be the prizefighter James Figg. On Tom's right, a landscape gardener identified as Charles Bridgeman, a member of Lord Burlington's circle which Hogarth mocked obsessively throughout his career, presents his plans, suggesting that Tom has acquired a country seat. The rest of the entourage is made up of a dancing master, whose French origins are betrayed by his affected pose and extravagant dress, a huntsman blowing his horn, a jockey who brandishes a trophy awarded at Epsom to his mount 'Silly Tom', and a hired bruiser, who apparently monopolizes the young rake's attentions. In the background, yet more tradesmen wait their turn to be received by the spendthrift rake.

The shallowness of our hero's pretension to gentility is testified by the pictures which decorate the room: two portraits of fighting cocks incongruously flank an old master painting, typical of the works accumulated by 'false' connoisseurs which so incensed Hogarth. Its subject — the Judgement of Paris — ironically echoes the transaction being conducted by Tom. His interest in the bruiser says little for his wisdom and bodes ill for his future.

# A Rake's Progress: 2. The Rake's Levée

*Painted 1733-34*
*62.23 x 74.93 cm*
*Sir John Soane's Museum, London*

It is three o'clock in the morning, as we can tell from the pocket watch which the two prostitutes have succeeded in removing from Tom's jacket. Amidst a scene of drunkenness and depravity, the young rake lies prostrate, glass in hand, his clothes in total disarray and his sword hanging precariously from his belt, where he has apparently thrust it following a brawl with a night watchman, whose lamp lies near his feet.

The Rose Tavern, scene of Tom's debauchery, was a notorious haunt of prostitutes and criminals near Drury Lane, demolished in the 1770s to make way for an extension to the theatre. Strewn with broken glasses, dishes and furniture, it plays host to a tableau reminiscent of the parable of the Prodigal Son or classical bacchanalia. The sense of an anarchic inversion of values is driven home as a female reveller sets fire to a map of the world, while a set of portrait heads of Roman emperors decorating the room has been defaced — with the single exception of Nero, the most depraved of them all.

In the foreground, a girl disrobes in preparation for her routine as a 'posture woman'. The metal platter and candle being brought into the room by 'Leather Coat', a well-known porter at the tavern, form part of her act, during which she will dance naked on the table, striking various poses as she spins around on the plate.

Reminiscent of such portrayals of drunkenness in Hogarth's work as *A Midnight Modern Conversation* (*c.* 1730-31) and *An Election Entertainment* (page 121, 1753-54), the rake's behaviour here epitomizes the sin of luxury, a theme widely debated by contemporary polemicists who feared that national strength and commercial vigour would be sapped by private indulgence and neglect of public duty.

# A Rake's Progress: 3. The Rake at the Rose Tavern

*Painted 1733-34*
*62.23 x 74.93 cm*
*Sir John Soane's Museum, London*

The scene takes place in St James's, Westminster, in view of the palace. The leeks worn by two of the protagonists reveal that the date is 1 March, St David's Day, and also the birthday of Queen Caroline. It is to her levée that Rakewell is bound, dressed in his finery, in all probability to petition for a place as a means of shoring up his parlous financial state.

So extravagantly has he treated his bequest that Tom is already prey to creditors. His sedan chair has been waylaid by bailiffs and he gapes in astonishment as they press him to pay his outstanding debts. Somewhat melodramatically, Sarah Young, whom Tom spurned when he came into his fortune, is at hand to rescue her former lover. Now working as a seamstress (as we can see from the contents of the box which she has let fall to the ground), she pushes forward to offer her meagre resources to pay off Tom's debts. The scene is witnessed by a lamplighter, who is so absorbed by events that he spills his oil, 'anointing' the rake who, through a trick of perspective, apparently stands beneath him. Meanwhile, a young urchin in the foreground takes advantage of the commotion to make off with Tom's gold-topped cane.

In a later engraved version of this scene, Hogarth replaced the young thief with an unruly group of bootblacks, newspaper vendors and other children, playing cards and dice, while one of their number purloins Tom's handkerchief. In the background, White's gaming house is struck by lightning. Through such modifications, Hogarth alludes to the way of life which has brought about Tom's downfall.

# A Rake's Progress: 4. The Rake Arrested, Going to Court

*Painted 1733-34*
*62.23 x 74.93 cm*
*Sir John Soane's Museum, London*

In a vain attempt to recover his fortunes, the rake contracts a secret marriage with a one-eyed old woman, whose main appeal is evidently financial. The service takes place in the dilapidated surroundings of Marylebone Old Church, then on the edge of the city and popular for clandestine ceremonies. Its peeling walls and general air of neglect provide a fitting setting for such an evidently opportunistic, loveless match. Yet the inscription on the balcony records that in 1725 — less than ten years earlier — the interior had been renovated by churchwardens Thomas Sice and Thomas Horn, whose probity Hogarth evidently calls into question by depicting the church in such a rundown state. The charade of Christian charity practised in the parish is made clear by the threadbare coat worn by the charity-boy who places a hassock at the bride's feet. The creed is torn, the tablet inscribed with the Ten Commandments is cracked, and the Poor Box has received such infrequent use that it is shrouded in cobwebs.

As Tom holds out the wedding ring, he already eyes up his next potential conquest — the bridesmaid who adjusts the old woman's dress. Meanwhile, his past almost frustrates his plans for the future, as Sarah Young, bearing her child, attempts to enter the church and interrupt the service. Though her formidable mother sets about the pew opener, who fends her off with a bunch of keys, subsequent events demonstrate that the women were frustrated in their mission.

In the foreground, a pug (apparently modelled on the artist's dog Trump) courts a dog with one eye — an allusion to the main action reminiscent of the artist's symbolic use of animals in such works as *The Denunciation* (page 45) and the first scene of *Marriage à la mode* (page 99).

# A Rake's Progress: 5. The Rake Marrying an Old Woman

*Painted 1733-34*
*62.23 x 74.93 cm*
*Sir John Soane's Museum, London*

The chaos of the Rose Tavern takes on a different, more sinister complexion in this scene as Tom, driven to despair by his losses at the gaming table, descends into madness. Internal evidence in the engraved version of this scene situates the gaming house, like the tavern, in the notorious Covent Garden area. However, the fire engulfing the building — which the gamblers, obsessed with their gaming, apparently ignore — may allude to White's in St James's (depicted in an engraved version of *The Rake Arrested*), which had been the scene of a blaze in May 1733.

Hogarth displays a spectrum of reactions to gambling in this scene, ranging from the melancholic highwayman, dressed in his top coat and staring absently into space, who has apparently gambled away all his loot, to the figures in the background who have come to blows, probably over accusations of cheating. In the left-hand foreground a crusty-looking moneylender makes out an IOU to cover a loan to the well-dressed artistocrat ('Lord Cogg' in the print) who leans over him.

Tom has now exhausted such remedies, having squandered away two fortunes. Wigless, and with a frenzied expression on his face, he throws out his arms in despair, apparently cursing his fate. Clambering against his fallen chair, a black dog — symbol of depressive melancholy — barks at the raging figure.

# A Rake's Progress: 6. The Rake at a Gaming House

*Painted 1733-34*
*62.23 x 74.93 cm*
*Sir John Soane's Museum, London*

Confined to the Fleet debtors' prison (where Hogarth had passed a spell as a boy following the failure of his father's coffee house), Tom seems to have lost his senses. In a scene in which delusion plays a conspicuous role, he sits rigid with despair having received a rejection note for the play which lies rolled up on the table. A money-making project frustrated, he is hedged in by grasping hands, as the pot boy demands payment for ale and the turnkey wields his ledger and calls for his 'garnish money'. Tom's wife, emaciated and in rags, harangues her husband, wagging her finger and apparently shouting into his ear.

This scene of complete despair has proved too much for Sarah Young, who swoons from emotion as her dress is loosened and smelling salts are administered to restore her senses. The child anxiously tugging at Sarah's skirt is almost certainly Tom's daughter, her age signifying the passage of time since the rake's marriage in the fifth scene.

Around the cell are the remains of various money-making schemes — all as implausible as Tom's — by which various inmates have attempted to marshal the resources to secure their release. In the background, an alchemist is shown hard at work at his forge, whose furnace glows vividly in the midst of the gloom; various crucibles stand on a shelf next to a sheaf of papers (bearing the word 'philosophical' in the engraved version); a telescope protrudes through the window next to the furnace chimney; a pair of wings lies abandoned on top of the bed against which Sarah swoons, while the strangely dressed man helping her drops a scroll which, in the engraving, reads 'Being a New Scheme for paying ye Debts of ye Nation by T:L: now a prisoner in the Fleet'.

# A Rake's Progress: 7. The Rake in Prison

*Painted 1733-34*
*62.23 x 74.93 cm*
*Sir John Soane's Museum, London*

Now confined to the paupers' asylum, Bethlem Hospital, Tom has finally lost his grip on sanity. Borrowing the rake's pose from the stone figures of melancholy and raving madness by Caius Gabriel Cibber which once decorated the hospital's entrance gate, Hogarth groups Tom with the ever-loyal Sarah and a hospital attendant in a tableau reminiscent of the standard iconography of the Lamentation. At the nadir of his delusive journey from riches to poverty and mental turmoil, Hogarth finally shows Rakewell as an object of pathos, if not of dignity.

Under the condescending eye of the fashionable ladies who have visited the hospital to be diverted by its inmates, Hogarth presents a complex panorama of delusive personalities, some of whom demonstrate character flaws reminiscent of Tom's own. The cells are populated by a religious fanatic, gazing adoringly at a wooden cross, and a man mad with pride, naked apart from his crown, who brandishes his sceptre and urinates against the wall. Scarcely visible in the painting, a figure behind his door calculates longitudes on the wall, while a mad astronomer, gazing at the invisible heavens through a roll of paper, crouches next to a mad tailor with a tape measure in front of him. On the left, a musician plays his violin with his music draped over his wig, while behind him a figure sits stiffly in a make-shift mitre pretending to be Pope and a melancholic lover by his side stares gloomily into space .

Like the heroine in *A Harlot's Progress* (see pages 20-22), the rake pays the price for his attempt to rise in the world through illegitimate means. A victim of luxury and loose living, he is presented by Hogarth as a warning that only true merit and hard work can lead to durable prosperity and happiness in Hanoverian England.

# A Rake's Progress: 8. The Rake in Bedlam

*Painted 1733-34*
*62.23 x 74.93 cm*
*Sir John Soane's Museum, London*

Upon learning of the intention to employ the Venetian Jacopo Amigoni to decorate their staircase and great hall, Hogarth approached the authorities of St Bartholomew's Hospital in 1734, offering his own services free of charge. Over the next three years, he produced two substantial oils for the staircase, both of which feature biblical scenes of charity and healing. Though *The Good Samaritan*, completed in 1737, is relatively disappointing, the earlier scene of Christ curing the sick at the Pool of Bethesda displays an accomplishment which belies the fact that this was Hogarth's first attempt at a monumental historical composition.

Working with his friend, the landscapist George Lambert, Hogarth illustrates an episode from John 5: 2-9 in which Christ comes upon a lame man at a pool in Jerusalem reputed for its miraculous curative powers. Ignored by others seeking relief, the lame man sits at the pool's edge, unable to reach the restorative waters, until Christ encounters him and commands him: 'Rise, take up thy bed, and walk.'

Hogarth's rendition of this scene combines a pictorial style owing much to Italian precedent with a veristic concern for physiological accuracy. In particular, the artist carefully details the symptoms of the figures around the pool, allowing the viewer to infer the disease from which each is suffering. The depiction of such ailments as rickets (first described by Dr Glisson at St Bartholomew's in 1650), gout, obesity and blindness lends an unambiguously contemporary resonance to this work of historical reconstruction.

Admired by George Vertue as a 'great work of painting [which] is by every one judged to be more than coud be expected of him', Hogarth's mural substantiated his claim that English artists were more than capable of excelling in the higher genres, which the nation's patrons normally entrusted to continental competitors.

# The Pool of Bethesda

*Painted 1736*
*416.5 x 617.2 cm*
*St Bartholomew's Hospital, London*

Hogarth produced the canvases which make up the suite of *The Four Times of Day* at the request of Jonathan Tyers, who opened his pleasure gardens at Vauxhall in 1732. Copies made after the works by Francis Hayman decorated the pavilions there, as did a replica of *The Enraged Musician* (1741) and the artist's history piece *Henry VIII and Anne Boleyn* (1729, now lost), which according to Horace Walpole hung in the Prince's Pavilion. The artist's work for Tyers was rewarded with the gift of a gold entrance ticket for the gardens.

Unusually, the *Four Times* sequence does not follow the adventures of a particular individual or group, but juxtaposes different street scenes occurring in or around London in the morning, at noon, in the evening and at night. While the first scene is situated in Covent Garden, familiar from such works as *The Rake at the Rose Tavern* (page 69), succeeding episodes are sited outside St-Giles'-in-the-Fields, by Sadler's Wells (a resort which directly competed with Tyers's establishment), and near Charing Cross. Nor do the episodes take place on a single day: while Covent Garden is covered in snow, the evening scene is staged in high summer, and the final episode occurs in late May.

Hogarth sets the scene for *Morning* in front of Inigo Jones's St Paul's church, straining topographical accuracy by depicting the disreputable Tom King's Tavern, an all-night haunt for prostitutes and their clients, on the west side of the piazza. On a bitterly cold morning, revellers and beggars mix in the foreground, seeking warmth in physical contact or from the flames of a small fire. Only the sour-looking prude on her way to church seems immune to the frost, her frigid disposition contrasting with the earthy sensuality of the women she looks upon with such disapproval.

# The Four Times of Day: Morning

*Painted 1736-38*
*73.6 x 60.96 cm*
*Bearsted Collection, The National Trust , Upton House*

Situated outside a French chapel in Hog Lane, just off Charing Cross Road, *Noon* offers a contrast in temperaments as striking as that which provides the central theme in *Morning*. The congregation is made up of conspicuously sober and sour-faced members, most of whom are drably dressed and undemonstrative. They are upstaged by the foreground trio — possibly a married couple with their son — who are clothed in high French style and indulge in a display of affected grace which contrasts amusingly with the old ladies greeting each other on the extreme left-hand side of the canvas.

Two taverns stand opposite the chapel on the other side of the street, representing sensual pleasure, just as Tom King's had done in *Morning*. The black man molesting the serving girl who is carrying a pie outside the *Baptist's Head* recalls the robust sensuality of King's clients in *Morning*, as well as echoing the chaste embrace of the old ladies in front of the chapel. Similarly, the mop-headed boy who stands crying as the contents of his dish spill on to the ground forms a piquant contrast with the dandified young lad whose powdered wig, sword and cane epitomize the affectation of the French. Behind this group, in an upstairs window of the *Good Woman* (good since headless — and hence silent), a domestic dispute provokes the lady of the house to pitch her husband's lunch into the street below. The robust sensuality of the English, symbolized in terms of diet, sexuality and plain speaking is thus juxtaposed with the brittleness and aridity of their French neighbours.

# The Four Times of Day: Noon

*Painted 1736-38*
*74.93 x 62.23 cm*
*The Trustees of the Grimsthorpe and*
*Drummond Castle Trust*

This witty and animated conversation piece portrays John, Lord Hervey — who stands towards the centre of the composition pointing at an architectural plan — in the company of a group of friends and political allies, all of whom were supporters of Sir Robert Walpole. The scene is set at Maddington, the shooting lodge owned by Stephen and Henry Fox, who are shown socializing with the third Duke of Marlborough and Thomas Winnington. The most extraordinary motif is provided by the Reverend Wilman, who stands perched on a chair behind Stephen Fox, gazing at a distant church through a telescope, apparently oblivious to his imminent fall. As a representative of divine wisdom, apparently out of place in decidedly secular company, he is counterbalanced by the symbol of earthly wisdom, Minerva, whose statue on the right seems to follow Wilman's gaze towards the hill.

The male bonding which forms the theme of this work has led to it being read in the light of contemporary anti-Walpole satire, which frequently made veiled allusions to homosexuality in Whig circles. In his *Epistle to Dr Arbuthnot* of 1735, Alexander Pope presented the bisexual Hervey in the guise of 'Sporus' — 'This painted Child of Dirt that stinks and stings' — while his relationship with Walpole was described by William Pulteney as similar to 'a certain unnatural, reigning vice (indecent and almost shocking to mention)'. In this respect, the conspicuous gateposts and walking sticks may be considered as harbouring potentially phallic overtones. Be that as it may, the overall frivolity of this genteel open-air conversation scene suggests a light-hearted contrast between the sacred and the profane, in which virtue seems precariously positioned.

# Lord Hervey and His Friends

*Painted c. 1738*
*127 x 101 cm*
*The National Trust, Ickworth House, Suffolk*

One of the most remarkable women of her age, Mary Edwards was Hogarth's most devoted patron during the 1730s, commissioning a number of portraits, a conversation piece and the satirical *Taste in High Life* (1742), as well as purchasing the oil version of *Southwark Fair* (1733). This striking portrait was completed some three years before her death in 1743.

Mary Edwards's enthusiasm for Hogarth's work was sustained by the enormous fortune she had inherited in 1728 when she was only twenty-four from her father Francis Edwards of Welham. Earning her an annual income of £50,000–£60,000, this inheritance left Edwards vulnerable to fortune-hunting suitors, hoping to take advantage of the absence of any legal protection for married women's property. Edwards's marriage at a clandestine Fleet wedding in 1731 to Lord Anne Hamilton (whom his father, the fourth Duke of Hamilton, had christened after the child's godmother, Queen Anne) turned out to be a disaster. Her new husband, five years her junior, proved profligate and unreliable. In order to protect the inheritance of her son Gerard Anne, Edwards took advantage of the secrecy with which she had married, and had all evidence of the wedding removed from the records, preferring to court disapproval as a single mother rather than see her husband squandering her fortune. Having escaped from this disastrous relationship, Mary Edwards recovered control over her financial affairs, which she administered independently until her death.

Hogarth's portrait, notable for the vivid red of Edwards's dress, was painted when the sitter was in her late thirties. The device of the dog, staring devotedly at his mistress, is a common feature of such works, signifying fidelity or admiration, though it is more often associated with male subjects. Its presence perhaps gives us a hint of Edwards's proud self-reliance.

## Miss Mary Edwards

*Painted c. 1740*
*125.4 x 96.2 cm*
*The Frick Collection, New York*

Provoked by the arrival in London of the French portraitist Jean-Baptiste Van Loo in December 1737, Hogarth produced this, his first essay in grand manner portraiture, 'without the practice of having done thousands, which every other face painter has before he arrives at doing as well'. The artist's characteristic immodesty is justified by this seminal work, which vies with the glamour of continental baroque portraiture, whilst moderating its ostentation to produce a more domesticated and approachable icon of middle-class Englishness.

Born in Lyme Regis, Thomas Coram had spent much of his adult life in America, where he had pursued a successful career in shipbuilding. Upon his return to England in around 1719, he became actively involved in philanthropic projects, most famously the Foundling Hospital in London which today bears his name. It was through his close association with this enterprise that Hogarth donated his services to portray Coram, whom he shows displaying the royal charter granted to the hospital in 1739.

In his everyday dress and somewhat neglected appearance, Coram embodies the image of bluff Englishness which stood in symbolic contrast to the effete ways of mainland Europe. Amidst the standard trappings of baroque portraiture — the column, draperies, ocean vista and allegory of Charity faintly visible on the right — Coram perches on a raised dais, his feet scarcely touching the ground. His unidealized features, ruddy complexion and open gaze convey a directness uncommon in the genre. Uncommon too is the way that Hogarth subtly undermines the illusion of ideal space by including the reflection of a window pane on the brilliant surface of the globe, which itself serves to remind the viewer of Coram's trading exploits. With 'this mighty portrait', as the artist himself described it, Hogarth graduated from the conversation piece to the grand style with almost casual ease.

# Captain Thomas Coram

*Painted 1740*
*283.7 x 147.3 cm*
*The Thomas Coram Foundation for Children, London*

The Royal Charter

Painted and given by W<sup>m</sup> Hogarth 1740.

At once an ambitious group portrait, painted life-size, and a complex emblem on art, innocence and the transience of childhood, *The Graham Children* is one of Hogarth's most accomplished works. Commissioned by Daniel Graham, apothecary to the royal household and the Chelsea Hospital, the portrait brings together his three children by his second marriage to Mary Crisp — the infant Thomas, the seven-year-old Henrietta Catherine, and Richard Robert, then aged eight — together with his wife's daughter from a previous marriage, Elizabeth, who is dressed in blue. The informality of the work, evident also in the contemporaneous *McKinnon Children* (National Gallery of Ireland, Dublin) provides a striking contrast to the stiffness and restraint typical of depictions of children at this period, and looks forward to the greater freedom found in family pieces by later Georgian artists such as Reynolds, Zoffany and Lawrence.

The emblematic content of the painting represents childhood as a fragile interlude protected from the hardships of the outside world, here represented by the predatory cat greedily stalking the caged goldfinch. Oblivious to the cat's evil intent, Richard Robert plays a serinette decorated with a scene of Orpheus, the first artist, charming the beasts with his music. He smiles at the finch's agitated singing, unaware that fear of attack has roused the bird. Between her fingers Elizabeth holds two cherries, the 'fruit of paradise' associated with childhood, while behind her a clock is decorated with a figure of Cupid, who holds Time's scythe to recall the ultimate triumph of Time over Love. The poignant message of the work, ultimately sombre in its reminder of mortality, derives from the recent death of the Grahams' young son Thomas, whom Hogarth here represents in a posthumous portrait.

# The Graham Children

*Painted 1742*
*192.4 x 205 cm*
*National Gallery, London*

This unfinished sketch is generally recognized as the final scene in Hogarth's abortive series *The Happy Marriage*, which was apparently intended as a contrast to the tale of marital disaster recounted in *Marriage à la mode* (pages 99-109). Only four of the original suite of works survive (*The Staymaker*, Tate Gallery, London; *The Wedding Banquet*, Royal Institute of Cornwall, Truro; *The Marriage Procession*, Collection of Marquess of Exeter), but it seems as if the artist projected a narrative of rural romance in which a young squire's courtship was shown as culminating in peace and contentment. Here, the tenants and gentry are entertained in the local manor house, following the hero's inheritance of his father's estate. A vivid rendition of movement, applied to an exotically varied array of physical types from the gangling fop to the portly squire, the work formed the basis for the second plate in *The Analysis of Beauty*, published in 1753.

Hogarth's abandonment of *The Happy Marriage* illustrates his uneasiness with episodes lacking moral tension. His preference for mordant irony and social criticism frustrated the novelist Samuel Richardson's proposal for him to provide illustrations to *Pamela*. Hogarth himself resumed the difficulty in *The Analysis of Beauty*, where he remarks:

*It is strange that nature hath afforded us so many lines and shades to indicate the deficiencies and blemishes of the mind, whilst there are none at all that point out the perfections of it beyond the appearance of common sense and placidity. Deportment, words, and actions must speak the good, the wise, the witty, the humane, the generous, the merciful, and the brave. Nor are gravity and solemn looks always a sign of wisdom.*

# The Country Dance

*Painted c. 1745*
*68.58 x 90.17 cm*
*Tate Gallery, London*

This monumental portrait, commissioned by Mr Duncombe of Duncombe Park for the then unprecedented figure of £200, records a moment from the immensely successful production of *Richard III*, staged by Garrick at Goodman's Fields theatre in 1741. In the same way that Garrick's performance marked an important step in the eighteenth-century revival of Shakespeare, so Hogarth's work represents a crucial development in the evolution of history painting during the period.

Hogarth shows Garrick in the tent scene (Act 5, scene 3) when Richard, on the eve of Bosworth Field, wakes in terror, haunted by thoughts of his former victims. Richard cries out:

*Give me another horse! bind up my wounds!*
*Have mercy, Jesu! Soft! I did but dream.*
*O coward conscience, how dost thou afflict me!*

Hogarth's portrayal, which draws on Le Brun's celebrated *Family of Darius before Alexander the Great*, shows the halting steps by both actors and artists to achieve an historically exact rendering of the past. Though such an accessory as armour, specially loaned from the Tower of London, is included in the left foreground, and Garrick is shown without his wig, his vaguely Elizabethan costume points to the relatively approximate sense of period which still dominated the British stage.

Famed for his 'naturalistic' acting style, Garrick is displayed frozen with fear in a pose familiar from pictorial manuals on gesture and expression, a source widely used by Georgian actors to achieve appropriate dramatic effect. Midway between a theatrical portrait and an historical rendering of an episode from the nation's past, Hogarth's work offers a fascinating insight into eighteenth-century actors' stagecraft. At the same time, it represents an important episode in the pictorial reconstruction of British history which so preoccupied both Hogarth's contemporaries and his successors.

# David Garrick as Richard III

*Painted 1745*
*190.5 x 250 cm*
*Walker Art Gallery, Liverpool*

Announcing the imminent completion of his new series of comic history paintings to the young Joshua Reynolds, Hogarth reputedly exclaimed: 'I shall very soon be able to gratify the world with such a sight as they have never seen equalled.' His bullish tone was matched by the care he lavished on the paintings, now treated as independent works rather than merely as a prepararatory step in producing finished prints, and by the assiduity with which he sought French artists to undertake the engraving on his behalf. Advertising the forthcoming prints in April 1743 the artist emphasized: 'Particular care will be taken, that there may not be the least Objection to the Decency or Elegancy of the whole Work, and that none of the Characters represented shall be personal.'

Though fictional, Hogarth's central characters were inspired by the increasing vogue for marital alliances between old aristocratic families and wealthy members of the commercial bourgeoisie — an arrangement which traded reflected social prestige for hard cash. Here, the elegant Lord Squanderfield proudly points to the family's lineage, which extends back to William the Conqueror. He accepts a pile of banknotes from the ungainly, unfashionably dressed merchant, and exchanges them for the mortgage documents proffered by an emaciated usurer. Through the window, we see the cause of the Earl's financial embarrassment: an incomplete Palladian mansion on which he has dissipated his fortune.

Meanwhile, the future couple display mutual indifference as the Earl's foppish son gazes admiringly at his own reflection, while his fiancée plays with her handkerchief and succumbs to the blandishments of the smooth-talking lawyer Silvertongue. Apart from the over-blown French baroque portrait of the Earl, the pictures decorating the room feature scenes of violence and conflict — David decapitating Goliath, Judith holding Holofernes's severed head, the Medusa — providing a portent to future events.

## Marriage à la mode: 1. The Marriage Contract

*Painted 1743-45*
*69.6 x 90.8 cm*
*National Gallery, London*

It is 1.20 a.m., and the young Earl has just returned from a night on the town. A woman's bonnet protruding from his pocket attracts the dog's attention with its unfamiliar scent, while his sword lies broken on the floor, apparently damaged in a brawl. His wife stretches in exhaustion after a strenuous evening's card playing; a copy of *Hoyle on Whist* lies open at her feet, while cards are strewn on the floor in the far room. The division between the couple is stressed by their physical isolation from each other, accentuated by the intervening table, and by the self-absorbed state in which each is wrapped. The household's financial difficulties are made plain in the despairing gesture of the steward, who clutches a wad of unpaid bills and carries a ledger under his left arm.

The interior decoration of the couple's home serves as an emblem of their unsatisfactory relationship. The fireplace is in the style of the architect William Kent, Hogarth's *bête noire*, whose neo-Palladianism was a frequent butt of the artist's satire (as in the incomplete mansion featured in the previous scene). The ornaments on the mantelpiece are a thoughtlessly eclectic mix — a Roman bust with a broken nose is flanked by a jumble of glass jars, ornaments and Indian figurines. Behind the bust, a decorative canvas features Cupid playing the bagpipes amidst ruins, his bow unstrung. The wall clock is a grotesque cocktail of rococo and chinoiserie, topped by two incongruous-looking fish under the watchful eye of a seated cat. The picture collection in the far room continues the sense of haphazard indifference with which the house has been decorated: portraits of apostles share a wall with a painting so obscene that it is shielded from view by a curtain. Such accumulated detail underlines the newlyweds' anomie.

## Marriage à la mode: 2. Early in the Morning

*Painted 1743-45*
*69.6 x 90.8 cm*
*National Gallery, London*

This macabre scene is situated in the 'museum' in St Martin's Lane of the quack Doctor Misauban, whom Hogarth had previously satirized in the fifth plate of the *Harlot's Progress* (see page 22). Amongst the curiosities on display, Hogarth reveals a skeleton making amorous advances on an anatomical model in the cupboard behind the seated Earl. The cupboard is topped by a strange, glaring head with a pill in its open mouth, flanked by a sample bottle and a tripod, with a giant femur on the wall behind. Overhead, an ostrich's egg is suspended from the belly of a stuffed crocodile. The rest of the room is filled with the doctor's 'tools of the trade': an array of glass jars on the left wall contain his dubious cures, while the gruesome machine on the right is described in the open book resting on it as being for either resetting dislocated shoulders or removing a cork from a bottle.

The young Earl's visit to this dubious doctor is a result of the womanizing in the previous scene. As the patches covering the sores on his neck reveal, the Earl has contracted syphilis, and is now confronting Misauban with the pills he apparently purchased from the bawd, who glares angrily at the young man and opens a knife. At his side, a demure young girl holding a pill box dabs at her lip, suggesting that she too is afflicted and may, indeed, be the source from whom the Earl has picked up the disease.

Though the narrative here is rather less easily deciphered than in many similar works by Hogarth — and provoked a degree of confusion amongst contemporary commentators — the crucial fact of the Earl's ailment is beyond doubt, and demonstrates the way in which Hogarth associates misconduct with retributive effect.

# Marriage à la mode: 3. The Inspection

*Painted 1743-45*
*69.6 x 90.8 cm*
*National Gallery, London*

Reminiscent of the second scene of *The Rake's Progress* (page 67) both through its setting and in its theme of bourgeois imitation of aristocratic manners, *The Toilette* shows the Countess surrounded by a group of parasites who resemble Tom Rakewell's entourage. As she has her hair dressed by a barber who, judging from his pigtail, his profession and his emaciated appearance, is probably French, she is serenaded by an Italian castrato — usually recognized as the mezzo-soprano Senesino, a singer at the King's Theatre, Haymarket. A group of foolishly foppish guests sit idly drinking tea and exchanging gossip while the lawyer Silvertongue makes an assignation with the Countess, pointing to a scene of a masquerade which decorates the screen behind the sofa on which he reclines.

Though she is now a mother (as the child's rattle hanging from her chair reveals), the Countess apparently enjoys an active social life. Invitations are strewn on the floor by the singer's feet, while an open catalogue in the bottom right-hand corner of the canvas indicates that she has recently attended an auction sale — a venue regarded with suspicion by some contemporaries. The turbanned boy pulls one of her purchases from a basket — a figure of Actaeon, whose horns allude to the fate which has befallen the cuckolded Earl.

Works of art more generally pass testimony on the moral depravity of the household. Above the screen, we see Lot being debauched by his daughters next to a portrayal of the rape of Io. Behind the flautist on the left Correggio's *Rape of Ganymede* (previously used in *The Marriage Contract*, page 63) is surmounted by a portrait of Silvertongue, the object of the Countess's adulterous affections.

# Marriage à la mode: 4. The Toilette

*Painted 1743-45*
*70.5 x 90.8 cm*
*National Gallery, London*

In a scene reminiscent of the Deposition of Christ, the Earl falls to the floor, having lost his life in a duel with Silvertongue, whom he has caught red-handed with his wife at the Turk's Head bagnio. The lawyer, dressed only in his nightshirt, scrambles through the window while the night watch bursts through the door, stunned by the scene which awaits them. The Countess, like a repentant Magdalen, clasps her hands in supplication amidst her discarded clothes and a face mask from the evening's earlier entertainment.

Again, Hogarth uses paintings and interior decoration to provide ironic commentary on the action. Above the door, St Luke seems to stare into the room, holding his pencil and drawing board, in readiness to capture the Virgin's likeness. Yet the scene of adultery and murder he witnesses before him has little to do with virginity. On the back wall, a tapestry of the Judgement of Solomon alludes to the protagonists' fate, while a grotesque portrait of a prostitute posing as a shepherdess seems to mock the events played out before her. In a twist of irony, Hogarth frames the dying Earl's head against a mirror on the back wall, a poignant reference to the opening scene in the sequence where the young man preened himself while his fiancée became acquainted with his future killer.

# Marriage à la mode: 5. The Death of the Earl

*Painted 1743-45*
*69.6 x 90.8 cm*
*National Gallery, London*

The series comes full circle, closing in the home of the merchant, with its view over London Bridge, just as the sequence opened in the Earl's apartments overlooking his mansion. With its simple furnishings and vulgar Dutch paintings, the interior suggests a frugality as extreme as the Earl's extravagance. The uncarpeted floor, broken windows, emaciated dog and unappetizing meal collude to evoke a miserliness reminiscent of Rakewell's father in *The Rake's Progress*.

It is in these inauspicious surroundings that the Countess's life has come to an end. As the broadside lying at her feet confirms, Silvertongue has been hanged for murder. In despair, his former lover has procured a phial of laudanum, which now lies empty on the floor, and has taken her own life. As her miserly father salvages her wedding ring before the onset of rigor mortis, the doctor can be seen leaving in the hall on the left. Meanwhile, the apothecary, the handle of whose stomach pump protrudes from his jacket pocket, reprimands the simple-minded servant for having fetched the poison for the Countess.

In a final embrace, the Countess's child kisses the prostrate corpse. Leg irons reveal that the child suffers from rickets, a disease which eighteenth-century commentators associated with over-indulgence rather than deprivation – like gout, from which the old Earl suffers in the opening scene. The black spot on the child's cheek also betrays the signs of syphilis passed on by the young Earl. The congenital handicaps inflicted on the child by parental misdeeds are compounded, in a final irony, by the fact that the child is a girl: the family tree, so proudly brandished by the Earl in the opening scene, has withered and will die.

## Marriage à la mode: 6. The Death of the Countess

*Painted 1743-45*
*69.6 x 90.8 cm*
*National Gallery, London*

Hogarth produced three self-portraits during his career — an unfinished head-and-shoulders study in the mid-1730s; the present work, completed shortly after *Marriage à la mode*; and a small full-length of the artist painting the Comic Muse (1758, page 42). Both this late emblematic work and the 1745 portrait provided the basis for engravings which the artist appended as a frontispiece to bound folios of his prints. Both thus serve to some degree as manifestoes, or distillations of the artist's preferred public persona.

Typically of Hogarth, the 1745 portrait is a conceit; rather than presenting an ostensibly unmediated likeness (as he had attempted in the vigorously painted early study), the artist portrays himself as a representation. This is a picture within a picture, though one in which 'illusion' and 'reality' sustain an apparent continuity through the drape which seems to swathe the 'fictive' painter before sweeping up in a steep diagonal to the top right-hand corner.

The junction between these two registers is concealed by the artist's pug dog, Trump. One of three such animals owned by Hogarth over the course of his career, the pug became something of a trademark, featuring in several works, most notably the late satire on the radical polemicist Charles Churchill, *The Bruiser* (1763), a reworking of the present portrait in which the dog ostentatiously urinates on the highly unflattering *Epistle to Hogarth*, a satirical poem published by this henchman of John Wilkes at the height of the Bute affair.

Next to the dog, a palette is inscribed with the serpentine Line of Beauty, which was given pride of place in *The Analysis of Beauty*, the theoretical tract which Hogarth issued in 1753. The pile of books on which the portrait rests — Swift, Milton and Shakespeare — confirms the literary standing of Hogarth the 'comic history painter'.

# Self-Portrait with Pug

*Painted 1745*
*90 x 70 cm*
*Tate Gallery, London*

Amongst the 375 governors of the Foundling Hospital, no fewer than 20 were artists, and it was largely at Hogarth's behest that a group of painters freely offered their services to decorate the hospital's premises when it was decided that money could not be made available for such a purpose from the charity's funds. The most conspicuous result of this initiative was a series of history paintings, all drawing on Old Testament stories of abandoned children, that was donated to the hospital's Court Room in 1747 by Hayman, Highmore, Wills and Hogarth.

This act of largesse was not entirely disinterested, since such a prestigious venue provided English artists with a much-needed opportunity to display their skills to a fashionable metropolitan public. Indeed, the Foundling Hospital soon became a noted sight which, with works by artists such as Ramsay, Gainsborough, Reynolds and Wilson, functioned as the city's first permanent gallery. In recognition, artists dined annually at the hospital on the anniversary of William III's landing in England, 5 November, a tradition that proved seminal in the development of formal artistic institutions in England.

Hogarth's contribution to the scheme complements Hayman's *Finding of Moses*, and shows the young prophet brought before his adoptive mother by his nurse — the woman who is, in fact, his natural mother — whom a servant pays off for her services. The work is curiously focused on Pharaoh's daughter, in her brilliant red robes, although her dominance somewhat unbalances the composition, which Hogarth had loosely based on Poussin's *The Child Moses treading the Pharaoh's Crown*. His attempt at local colour, with the miniature crocodile crouched in the foreground and his strange amalgamation of architectural styles, provides an undeniably approximate feel of ancient Egypt. Despite its deficiencies, however, the work was described by Vertue as giving 'most striking satisfaction and approbation'.

# Moses Brought before Pharaoh's Daughter

*Painted 1746*
*177.8 x 213.36 cm*
*The Thomas Coram Foundation for Children, London*

It was during his second visit to France in 1748 that Hogarth was arrested and deported by the military authorities, after he had been apprehended sketching the fortifications at Calais. His commemoration of this event in *Calais Gate*, which portrays the artist just as the long arm of the French law reaches out to trap him, is a classic distillation of contemporary British Francophobia.

Set against the city gate itself, constructed by the English during their occupation of the port during the middle ages, Hogarth presents a troop of Gallic stereotypes, typical of the under-nourished, ragged buffoons familiar in satirical depictions of the French by Georgian caricaturists. Their interest is aroused by the arrival of a sirloin of beef, destined for the establishment of Madame Grandsire, whose hotel catered for English visitors to the town. As the cook struggles beneath its weight, the portly friar scarcely conceals his gluttonous thoughts, while the sentinels — dining on the 'soupe maigre' which English commentators claimed was the staple diet of their less fortunate neighbours — stand wide-eyed in admiration and amazement. In the foreground, a wretched Scots Jacobite huddles in the shadows, his patched forehead covering wounds possibly inflicted during the 1745 uprising.

*Calais Gate* encapsulates Hogarth's claim that the French were characterized by 'poverty, slavery and insolence, with an affectation of politeness'. His views, typical of the age, equated French impoverishment with regal absolutism and the power of Catholicism (evident in the background vignette of priests parading the Host). The British, by contrast, were judged to owe their superior prosperity, and more substantial cuisine, to the freedom of the subject won in the Glorious Revolution of 1688 — an equation summed up in the motto of the Sublime Society of Beefsteaks, a club to which Hogarth belonged: 'Beef and Liberty'!

# Calais Gate, or O! The Roast Beef of Old England

*Painted 1748*
*78.94 x 95.6 cm*
*Tate Gallery, London*

Hogarth's greatest opportunity to demonstrate his skills as a history painter in the grand style came when he was approached by the Honourable Society of Lincoln's Inn to provide a major work for their hall. The chance arose thanks to a bequest of £200 from Lord Wyndham, formerly Chancellor of Ireland, and the good offices of Lord Mansfield, later Lord Chief Justice, who secured the commission for his friend Hogarth. In response, the artist selected a courtroom drama taken from the Acts of the Apostles, showing Paul defending himself against accusations of sedition levelled by Tertullus — shown on the left — at the instigation of the high priest Ananias, who sits immediately behind the apostle's adversary. The case is heard by Felix, governor of Judaea, with his Jewish wife, Drusilla, at his side.

Though the artist looked to the example of Thornhill's life of Saint Paul which decorates the cupola of Wren's cathedral, his main point of reference was the work of Raphael, and particularly the cartoons in the Royal Collection, which he probably studied through engravings. It is *Paul and the Blind Magician Elymas before Sergius Paulus* (Victoria and Albert Museum, London) which provided Hogarth with his main source, though for the figure of Paul he borrowed from the cartoon of *Paul preaching at Athens* from the same series. The result, though enormously ambitious, is not entirely convincing. The clogged composition and rather broadly drawn faces (reminiscent of the subsidiary figures in *Moses Brought before Pharaoh's Daughter*, page 113) suggests that such work, though allowing Hogarth to test his assertion that British painters were capable of rivalling the masters, scarcely exploits his natural strengths.

In a more congenial vein, Hogarth published a print burlesquing the scene in the manner of Rembrandt, a further dig at the connoisseurs' weakness for 'dismal dark subjects'.

# Paul before Felix

*Painted 1748*
*304.8 x 426.7 cm*
*Honorable Society of Lincoln's Inn, London*

Inspired by the Jacobite rebellion of 1745, *The March to Finchley* contrasts the chaotic tangle of thieving, drinking and whoring troops in the foreground with the disciplined lines of men setting out to defend the capital, who march away in the middle distance. Again, Hogarth raises the thorny issue of choice, embodied in the grenadier flanked by the two women in the centre of the composition: duty, reason and restraint are contrasted with disorder, sensual self-gratification and indulgence, Protestantism with Catholicism, patriotic sacrifice with betrayal of national honour.

The scene is set on the Tottenham Court turnpike, between the Adam and Eve on the left and the King's Head Tavern opposite — identified by the artist with the rebellious Stuart cause through its inn sign of Charles II, and with moral degradation through the horde of prostitutes gazing down on the mêlée below. The soldiers all seem to be the worse for their stop-over. Most stagger unsteadily, befuddled by drink, while one soldier in the right foreground has collapsed entirely, and is being plied with a restorative flask of gin by his over-enthusiastic comrade. Behind this group, another soldier alerts a pieman to the theft of milk from a maid whose attention has been diverted by an over-amorous guardsman. Meanwhile, he himself steals a tart from the pieman's tray.

Amidst this disorder, the anxious-looking grenadier carries the moral burden of the work. He is presented with a choice in the form of the young loyalist ballad seller on the left, who gestures pleadingly at her pregnant stomach, and the wildly gesturing crone who tugs him towards the brothel and brandishes Jacobite propaganda to attract his attention. Like Hercules at the crossroads, virtue and pleasure offer contrary paths, and duty is bidden to overcome ease.

# The March to Finchley

*Painted 1749-50*
*101.6 x 133.3 cm*
*The Thomas Coram Foundation for Children, London*

Though set in the fictional constituency of 'Guzzle-down', Hogarth's attack on the fatuousness and corruption of contemporary politics draws its inspiration from polling in Oxfordshire during the General Election of 1754. In common with many county constituencies in Hanoverian England, Oxfordshire was rarely contested during this period, since local magnates entered into private agreements to avoid the inconvenience of a sustained campaign. The Duke of Marlborough's challenge to this cosy arrangement in 1754 put the Tory incumbents on the defensive for the first time since 1710.

A parody of the Last Supper, *An Election Entertainment* displays the carnivalesque misrule triggered by the scramble for political office. While the Blues (Tory party) protest in the street against recent legislation to emancipate the Jews, the Orange (Whig) candidates offer food, drink and discreet bribes to win over the locals. Sir Commodity Taxem, the elegant beau being embraced by an ageing supporter, and his fellow candidate, harangued by a barber and a cobbler, appear overwhelmed by the riotous assembly over which they nominally preside. A Whig attorney, registering votes, collapses on to a pile of serving dishes after being struck on the head by a brick thrown through the window; the local mayor is bled by an apothecary to recover from a surfeit of oysters; a hired bruiser has a head wound cleaned with alchohol, while a young serving boy fills up a vat to ensure that the drink continues to flow freely. A defaced portrait of William III on the back wall suggests that the Tories have already used the room for a similarly disordered entertainment.

Hogarth's scene forms part of a rich tradition of caricatural representations of popular politics in the eighteenth century. Its animation and complexity makes it one of the artist's most accomplished and mordant works.

## An Election: 1. An Election Entertainment

*Painted 1753-54*
*101.6 x 127 cm*
*Sir John Soane's Museum, London*

Corruption and disorder thrive at the two party headquarters, lodged in neighbouring inns at the edge of town. In the foreground, the Tories have taken over The Royal Oak, partially concealing the inn sign with a banner attacking ministerial bribery. In the lower section Mr Punch, possibly an allusion to the Duke of Newcastle, showers supporters with gold coins scooped from a wheelbarrow. Above, money cascades from a window in the Treasury for distribution to ministerial supporters, while in the background the royal coach finds itself wedged under a low arch in the Horse Guards building — yet another squib at the expense of Hogarth's inveterate enemy, the architect William Kent.

Further down the road, the Whigs' headquarters at the Crown have been temporarily converted into an Excise Office. Irate Tories attack the building, and one of the mob attempts to saw off the signboard, foolishly oblivious to the fall he will suffer if he succeeds. The excise, a tax on wine and tobacco introduced by Walpole in 1733, was withdrawn under popular protest, though suspicions that taxation on commodities would be reintroduced lingered on.

Electoral malpractice abounds. Outside the inn, a Tory agent attempts to ingratiate himself with two women, offering them favours from a tray held by a Jewish pedlar, in the hope that they will sway their husbands' votes. The innkeeper's wife counts up bribes, perching on a figurehead representing the British lion swallowing a fleur-de lis. (In a 1757 engraved version, issued following the outbreak of the Seven Years' War, Hogarth removed the lion's vicious teeth.) A parody of Hercules's choice occupies centre stage, as a yeoman accepts bribes from representatives of both parties. On the right, a cobbler and a barber reminisce over past military glories, reliving the heroic sea battle of Portobello with fragments of clay pipes.

# An Election: 2. Canvassing for Votes

*Painted 1753-54*
*101.6 x 127 cm*
*Sir John Soane's Museum, London*

The public spectacle of polling — a process which often extended over many days — left ample scope for corruption. Here, Hogarth assembles a motley group of voters to discredit the sham which passed for a free election. In the foreground, a military veteran with a wooden leg and a missing right hand excites the anger of one of the parties' lawyers who challenges the validity of his oath, since he swears by placing his hook on the Bible. Behind him, the oath is taken by an imbecile, who is prompted by a figure wearing manacles on his legs and a Tory favour in his hat. The Whigs, not to be outdone, mount the stairs to the booth with a dying man in their arms, while a blind man and a cripple wait their turn to vote.

In the background, Hogarth untypically introduces an undisguised allegory in the shape of the coach, bearing the union flag in the escutcheon on its door. With its mountings broken, the coach threatens total collapse, but the footmen, absorbed in their game of cards, continue to ignore the warnings of their passenger, Britannia. Taken in conjunction with other references to national decline in the series, this vignette apparently serves as a warning that political negligence and mismanagement threaten England's future survival.

# An Election: 3. The Polling

*Painted 1753-54*
*101.6 x 127 cm*
*Sir John Soane's Museum, London*

The victory parade of the successful candidate is shown as a bizarre parody of Le Brun's *Battle of Granicus* in which the victorious Alexander the Great is replaced by the obese Whig parliamentarian George Bubb Doddington. As the supporters' signs confirm, he has been converted into a Tory by Hogarth. His selection for this somewhat precarious seat is made all the more ironic since Doddington, alone amongst prominent politicians, was defeated in 1754. In a mocking allusion to the eagle of victory which hovers over Alexander, Doddington is over-flown by a goose, which bears more than a passing resemblance to the politician.

A blind fiddler leads the parade, and fails to notice that it has been abruptly halted by a donkey, laden down with barrels of offal which have attracted the interest of a dancing bear. The bear's owner, a one-legged sailor, pays no attention to the animal's antics as he has become involved in a violent political dis-pute with a Tory supporter. His opponent's flail, swung over his shoulder to strike out at the sailor, hits one of the figures supporting the new member, who starts to topple from his seat. A woman is sent flying by a fleeing herd of 'Gadarene' swine and risks even greater discomfort when the parliamentarian lands upon her.

This anarchic scene is observed with some amuse-ment by the nobles feasting in the curious building on the left, one of whom — his back turned but wearing a distinctive wig — is quite probably the Duke of Newcastle. In an unglazed upper window, a lawyer draws up an indenture, suggesting that the whole contest between the parties has been a meaningless charade. The inscription on the sundail on the church wall 'Pulvis et umbra sumus' ('We are but dust and shadows') suggests world-weary contempt for such corruption.

# An Election: 4. Chairing the Members

*Painted 1753-54*
*101.6 x 127 cm*
*Sir John Soane's Museum, London*

This unusual image of Schutz paying the price of an evening's over-indulgence is thought to have been commissioned by his wife Susan Bacon, whom he had married in March 1755. The clue to the work's meaning lies in the inscription from Horace on the wall by the lyre: 'Vixi puellis nuper idoneus, &c' ('Not long ago I kept it in good order for the girls'). In the original ode, and through its positioning on Hogarth's canvas, the line refers to the lyre, which the poet claims to have hung up in the Temple of Venus after retiring from amorous adventures. In the present context, however, the epigram carries wider implications referring to Schutz's intemperance, and possible neglect of his marital duties.

The admonitory tone of this work pitches it midway between a genre painting and a portrait. The unusually frank intimacy of the scene apparently proved too strong for Schutz's descendants, who in the early nineteenth century had the work altered to show Francis Matthew blamelessly reading in bed. In its restored form, we can see Hogarth's directness in portraying bodily functions for moral effect — a scatalogical theme which, though unusual in painting, was ubiquitous in graphic satire of the period.

The Schutz family itself was related to the crown — Francis Matthew's father, Colonel John Schutz, was a second cousin of George II and had held a number of posts in the Hanoverian court. As Schutz himself was third cousin to Frederick, Prince of Wales, it has been suggested that Hogarth's commission for the work was possibly related to the late Prince's court circle at Leicester House.

# Francis Matthew Schutz in his Bed

*Painted c. 1755-60*
*63 x 75.5 cm*
*Norwich Castle Museum, Norfolk*

Painted with remarkable verve, acuity of observation and sympathy, this collective portrait, without parallel in the eighteenth century, demonstrates Hogarth's abiding interest in physiognomy and the deftness with which he was able to capture a likeness. Possibly finished in a single sitting, the work offers a more subdued, veristic contrast to the expressive heads which populate such plates as *Characters and Caricaturas* (1743, see page 15) or paintings such as *The Bench* (1758, page 135), and resembles the contemporaneous *Shrimp Girl* (page 2) in the effect of apparent spontaneity which it achieves. Hogarth's purpose in recording the features of a social class more normally conspicuous by their absence in eighteenth-century English art is unknown. Yet his theoretical preoccupation with the face and its expressive potential would suggest that his servants provided the artist with a convenient subject for what is essentially a virtuoso exercise in mimetic representation.

Hogarth's household had moved to the Golden Head, Leicester Fields in 1733, and the artist purchased a country retreat at Chiswick in 1749. Given the size of the Hogarth ménage, his retinue of servants was modest for the period. Other than the artist and his wife Jane, the extended family at this period consisted of his sister Anne, his mother-in-law Lady Thornhill, and his wife's companion, her young cousin Mary Lewis. Contemporary testimony records Hogarth's generosity as an employer, and apparently his servants tended to remain in service with the family over many years.

## Hogarth's Servants

*Painted mid-1750s*
*62.23 x 75.56 cm*
*Tate Gallery, London*

One of the most celebrated English actors of all time, David Garrick was a close personal friend of Hogarth, who portrayed him on several occasions, most notably in his celebrated role as Richard III in 1745 (page 97), and even designed the highly decorated chair in which he presided over meetings of the Shakespeare Club. Garrick greatly admired Hogarth, purchasing the paintings of the *Election* series (pages 121-127), organizing a subscription for the artist's tombstone and composing his epitaph, with the assistance of Samuel Johnson. Though Hogarth's portrait of the actor and his wife remains unfinished, it serves as an outstanding testament to the enduring affection which linked the two men.

Hogarth shows Garrick pausing for thought while he works on a prologue to Samuel Foote's comedy *Taste*. As he gazes dreamily into space, his wife, the dancer Eva Maria Veigel, playfully leans forward to pluck the pen from his fingers in a light-hearted subversion of the traditional theme of the (male) writer and the (female) Muse who lends him inspiration. The subject has been related to a portrait of the playwright Colley Cibber and his daughter, completed by the French artist Van Loo during his visit to England in the late 1730s (though now lost) — a further instance of Hogarth competing with a contemporary French prototype.

For whatever reason, Hogarth appears to have encountered difficulties with the work, altering such details as Garrick's eyes and right hand, and failing to finish the domestic interior in which the couple is set. A candle-snuffer above the actor's head, a book case, and prints and paintings decorating the room were outlined but not properly completed by the artist, leaving the elegant interplay of the two sitters perhaps all the more strikingly apparent.

# David Garrick and His Wife

*Painted 1757*
*17.4 x 18.1 cm*
*Royal Library, Windsor Castle*

Throughout his career Hogarth displayed particular interest in the human face and its infinite variety of expression. It was this fascination which inspired studies of the effect of particular emotions such as *The Laughing Audience* (1733) as well as such typological ensembles as *Scholars at a Lecture* (1736/7). It also informed portrait prints, like that of the Jacobite rebel Simon Lord Lovat (1746) or the radical politician John Wilkes (1763).

Here, in a late work, Hogarth returns to this abiding theme in his depiction of members of the Court of Common Pleas. Beneath their capacious wigs and robes, Hogarth has, in fact, portrayed several leading jurists of the period, most conspicuously the Chief Justice, Sir John Willes, a figure notorious for his immorality, whose hopes for preferment were frustrated by his evil reputation and stubborn vanity. On his right sits Henry Bathurst, later Lord Chancellor, and the two men are flanked by figures generally identified as William Noel and Sir Edward Clive.

Hogarth transformed the engraved version of this work into a personal manifesto, reminiscent in intent to *Characters and Caricaturas* of 1743 (see page 15). Adding a series of heads along the top of the print, beneath the image he appended a text in which he drew a sharp distinction between the pictorial rendition of character and the violation of physiognomic truth qualified as 'caracatura'. Describing the former as 'an Index of the mind, to express which with any degree of justness in Painting, requires the utmost Efforts of a great master', he scathingly dismissed caricature, the vogue for which had recently been imported to England from Italy. Likening caricatures to children's scribbling, he regarded them merely as 'a species of Lines that are produc'd rather by the hand of chance than of Skill', distinctive from his own highly wrought graphic style.

# The Bench

*Painted 1758*
*17.4 x 18.1 cm*
*Fitzwilliam Museum, Cambridge*

News that Hogarth was contemplating retirement prompted a generous commission for a final 'comic history painting' from the artist's friend the Irish peer Lord Charlemont. This elegant work, indebted to the example of such French masters as de Troy and Fragonard, reflects the cosmopolitanism of his patron's taste. An enthusiastic supporter of Hogarth, who had previously purchased *Calais Gate* (page 115) and the drawings for *The Four Stages of Cruelty,* Charlemont had amassed an impressive collection of French and Italian art, and was in the forefront of antiquarian studies, having travelled widely in Italy and Greece.

*The Lady's Last Stake,* inspired by Colley Cibber's comedy of the same title first produced in 1707, returns Hogarth to the theme of choice which had been a leitmotif in his work since such early projects as *The Beggar's Opera* and *A Harlot's Progress* (see pages 47 and 20-22). The artist himself described the scene as portraying 'a virtuous married lady that has lost all at cards to a young officer, wavering at his suit whether she should part with her honour or no to regain the loss which was offered to her'. The insistent young soldier holds out his winnings as he presses his suit. His intended victim turns away, though indecisively, shielding her face from the fire which blazes vigorously, consuming the playing cards which she has angrily thrown into the grate. An affectionate letter from her absent husband lies open on the floor by the hearth, a silent cipher of virtue counterbalancing the importunate blandishments of vice. The urgency of the decision is underlined by the clock on the mantelpiece, with its finial decoration of Cupid brandishing Time's scythe above the inscription 'Nunc, Nunc' ('Now, Now'). Time is running out, as the rising moon suggests, though the depiction of the Magdalene over the fireplace emphasizes the price of dishonour.

# The Lady's Last Stake

*Painted 1758-59*
*91.44 x 105.41 cm*
*Albright Knox Art Gallery, Buffalo, New York*

When a portrayal of Boccaccio's heroine Ghismonda, reputedly by Correggio though now attributed to the Florentine Furini, was sold at auction for £400, Hogarth's outrage was matched only by his conviction that he could do just as well. He therefore approached Sir Richard Grosvenor, one of the unsuccessful bidders, with a proposal for his own version of the subject, which would display modern British painters' capacity to rival, and even outshine the Old Masters so immoderately prized by the connoisseurs. So began one of the most unfortunate episodes in Hogarth's career.

The story of Ghismonda, most familiar to contemporaries through Dryden's reworking, 'Sigismunda and Guiscardo', in his *Fables Ancient and Modern* of 1699, was a particularly gruesome one. Sigismunda, a widow, falls in love with Guiscardo, and secretly marries him, in defiance of the wishes of her father, Tancred, Prince of Salerno. On learning of her disobedience, Tancred has Guiscardo murdered and sends a messenger to Sigismunda, bearing her husband's heart. Clutching it to her bosom, the young woman commits suicide in an act of heroic defiance.

It is this moment which Hogarth, following 'Correggio', shows here. 'My object,' he recorded, 'was dramatic and my aim to draw tears from the spectator.' Yet even a sympathetic contemporary such as Horace Walpole dismissed his Sigismunda as a 'maudlin strumpet', claiming that she had 'none of the sober grief, no dignity of suppressed anguish, no involuntary tear, no settled meditation on the fate she meant to meet, no amorous warmth turned holy by despair'. The pathetic, rather than heroic tone struck by Hogarth failed to please. Not only was Grosvenor unwilling to pay the extravagant asking price of £500, but Hogarth could not find another buyer for his work, and was forced to abandon plans for an engraved version.

## Sigismunda

*Painted 1759*
*99 x 125.73 cm*
*Tate Gallery, London*

# CHRONOLOGY

**1697**
10 November — Born in Bartholomew Close, Smithfield, London, fourth child of Richard Hogarth and Anne Gibbons. None of his older siblings had survived. A sister, Mary, is born in November 1699, and a second sister, Anne, in 1701.

**1707 or 1708**
Richard Hogarth's Latin-speaking coffee house fails and the family are confined to the Fleet prison for debtors.

**1712**
12 September — Act of amnesty: release of Hogarth family.

**1713**
2 February — Apprenticed to the silver engraver Ellis Gamble in Leicester Fields.

**1718**
11 May — Death of father, Richard Hogarth.

**1720**
April — Without completing his apprenticeship, Hogarth sets up as an engraver in the family home in Long Lane.
20 October — Joins Vanderbank's Academy in St Martin's Lane, training under John Vanderbank and Louis Chéron.

**1721**
Publishes his first satirical print, *The South Sea Scheme*.

**1722-23**
Works on book illustrations and trade cards. Attends Sir James Thornhill's free art academy; meets artist's daughter Jane.

**1724**
Publishes *Masquerades and Operas*, attacking the Burlington circle, and other satirical prints. Signs contract with Philip Overton for large *Hudibras* plates. Continues book illustration.

**1725**
Mary and Anne Hogarth, open a milliners in Long Walk, near St Bartholomew's. Publication of the satire on William Kent's altarpiece for St Clement Danes in September.

**1726**
February — Publication of large *Hudibras* prints.
April — Publication of small *Hudibras* prints.
27 December — Publishes *The Punishment of Lemuel Gulliver*, a satire on Sir Robert Walpole's ministry inspired by Swift's recent *Gulliver's Travels*.

**1727**
Starts to paint seriously.

**1728**
January — Opening of Gay's *Beggar's Opera*, inspiring the first of five paintings based on the play.

**1729**
23 February — Elopes with Jane Thornhill, and moves to Little Piazza, Covent Garden, near parents-in-law in Great Piazza.

Finishes work on *Beggar's Opera* series. Produces first comic genre scenes (*The Denunciation*) and establishes a reputation as a painter of conversation pieces.

**1730**
A scene of a prostitute waking up inspires Hogarth to complete his first narrative series, *A Harlot's Progress*.

**1731**
March — Hogarth announces his subscription for the prints of *A Harlot's Progress* which he undertakes to do himself.
Moves in, with wife, with Jane's parents in the Great Piazza.

**1732**
April — Publication of *A Harlot's Progress*; success marred by pirated versions. Authorizes set of cheap copies to combat this.
Commissions for conversation pieces: *The Cholmondeley Family* and *The Conquest of Mexico*.

**1733**
March — Paints a portrait of the murderess Sarah Malcolm, of whom he publishes an etching.
October — A request to paint the wedding of Anne, the Princess Royal is frustrated by the opposition of William Kent. Abortive commission for conversation piece of the royal family.

**1734**
February — Offers to decorate the staircase at St Bartholomew's Hospital.
25 July — Elected governor of St Bartholomew's Hospital.

**1735**
10 May — Death of mother, Anne Gibbons.
15 May — Royal assent granted to the Engravers' Copyright Act, prompted by Hogarth's campaign.
26 June — *A Rake's Progress* delivered to subscribers, though a pirated version has already appeared.
October — Founds St Martin's Lane Academy.

**1736**
April — Completes *Pool of Bethesda* for St Bartholemew's Hospital.

**1737**
Publishes *Scholars at a Lecture*, *The Distressed Poet* and *A Company of Undertakers*.
May — Launches subscription for *Four Times of Day* and *Strolling Actresses dressing in a Barn*.
9 June — Publishes essay defending Thornhill and British art, signed 'Britophil', after artist attacked in the *Daily Post*.
July — Completes *The Good Samaritan* for St Bartholomew's Hospital.

**1738**
May — Publishes *Four Times of Day* and *Strolling Actresses dressing in a Barn*.

**1739**
17 October — Founding Governor of the Foundling Hospital.

1740

May — Presents portrait of Captain Coram to the Foundling Hospital.

1741

20 November — Death of sister, Mary Hogarth.

1742

Begins paintings for *Marriage à la mode*. Portraits of the Graham and McKinnon children.

1743

April — Announces subscription to *Marriage à la mode*.

May — Visits Paris to hire engravers for *Marriage à la mode*.

1745

28 February — Holds auction of his comic history paintings.

May — Delivery of engraved version of *Marriage à la mode*.

1746

25 August — Publishes etching of the Jacobite rebel Simon Lord Lovat.

Works on *Moses brought before Pharaoh's Daughter* as part of a scheme to donate paintings to the Foundling Hospital.

1747

April — Exhibition of the history paintings decorating the Court Room at the Foundling Hospital.

October — Publication of *Industry and Idleness*.

5 November — First artists' dinner at the Foundling Hospital.

1748

June — Completion of *Paul before Felix* for Lincoln's Inn.

August — Trip to Paris but expelled by French authorities for drawing fortifications at Calais; paints *Calais Gate*.

1749

September — Buys country house in Chiswick.

Begins *The March to Finchley*.

1750

Subscription for engravings of *The March to Finchley*.

April – Lottery for the painting won by Foundling Hospital.

1751

February – Publishes *Beer Street*, *Gin Lane* and *The Four Stages of Cruelty*.

7 June — *Marriage à la mode* paintings raise only £120.

1752

February — Delivery of *Paul before Felix* engravings.

Begins work on *The Analysis of Beauty*.

1753

October — Split at the St Martin's Lane Academy.

November — Publication of *The Analysis of Beauty* provokes adverse press comment, but work itself generally well reviewed.

Begins work on *An Election*.

1755

22 February — *An Election Entertainment* published, though the other prints in the series are delayed until 1758.

May — Altarpiece commissioned for St Mary Redcliffe, Bristol.

December – Elected to the Society of Arts.

1756

March – *Invasion* prints published to boost morale after declaration of war with France.

August – Completion of St Mary Redcliffe commission.

1757

24 February — Announces that henceforth he will paint only portraits, leading to Lord Charlemont's commission for *The Lady's Last Stake*.

June — Appointed Serjeant Painter to the king.

Abandons Society of Arts over a disagreement in policy.

1758

26 April — Auction of Sir Luke Schaub's collection at which *Sigismunda*, attributed to Correggio, fetches over £400, a price which prompts Hogarth to undertake a version of the subject under commission from Sir Richard Grosvenor.

1759

June — Grosvenor rejects *Sigismunda*.

December — Begins *An Apology for Painters*, another defence of contemporary English artists.

1760

April — Exhibition of St Martin's Lane and Society of Arts from which Hogarth abstains.

Falls ill, recovering only the following spring.

1761

February — Exhibits *Sigismunda* as part of an abortive project for an engraving after the painting.

April — Contributes to an exhibition organized by the Society of Artists, a break-away group from the Society of Arts.

22 September — Coronation of George III.

October — Resignation of William Pitt and appointment of Lord Bute as head of ministry.

15 December — Elected to committee of Society of Artists.

1762

April - May — Sponsors signpainters' exhibition with Bonnell Thornton to satirize the Society of Arts' exhibition.

17 May — Society of Artists' exhibition opens; does not participate, suggesting a cooling of relations with the group.

9 September — Publishes pro-Bute print *The Times. Plate 1*, provoking a storm of abuse from Whig quarters.

25 September — Attacked by John Wilkes in the oppositional *North Briton*.

1763

7 April — Lord Bute resigns; work curtailed on *The Times. Plate 2*.

21 May — Publishes print of John Wilkes, currently charged with seditious libel for a reputed attack on the king in *North Briton*, no. 45.

30 June — Publication of Charles Churchill's attack on the

artist in his poetic *Epistle to William Hogarth.*
July — Struck by a paralytic seizure.
1 August — *The Bruiser,* an attack on Churchill.
1764
April — Publication of last print, *Tailpiece: The Bathos.*
June — Gives *Sigismunda* to James Basire to engrave.
16 August — Signs will.
25 October — Dies at his home in Leicester Fields.
2 November — Funeral at St Nicholas, Chiswick.

## SELECT BIBLIOGRAPHY

ANTAL, Frederick: *Hogarth and His Place in European Art,* Routledge and Kegan Paul, 1962.

ATHERTON, Herbert: *Political Prints in the Age of Hogarth: A Study of the Ideographic Representation of Politics,* Oxford University Press, 1974.

BINDMAN, David: *Hogarth,* Thames and Hudson, 1981.

BURKE, Joseph (ed): *William Hogarth. The Analysis of Beauty with rejected Passages from the Manuscript Drafts and Autobiographical Notes,* Clarendon Press, 1955.

COWLEY, Robert: *Marriage à-la-mode. A Re-view of Hogarth's Narrative Art,* Manchester University Press, 1983.

DABYDEEN, David: *Hogarth, Walpole and Commercial Britain,* Hansib, 1987.

LINDSAY, Jack: *Hogarth. His Art and His World,* Taplinger, 1977.

NICHOLS, John: *Anecdotes of William Hogarth, written by Himself: with Essays on His Life and Genius, and Criticisms of His Works,* 1833; reprint, Cornmarket Press, 1970.

PAULSON, Ronald: *Hogarth's Graphic Works: First Complete Edition,* 2 volumes. Yale University Press, 1965. Revised edition, 1989.

PAULSON, Ronald: *Hogarth: His Life, Times and Art,* 2 volumes. Yale University Press, 1971, abridged edition, 1974. A thoroughly revised version of this fundamental work is currently under publication in three volumes.

PAULSON, Ronald: *The Art of Hogarth,* Phaidon, 1975.

PAULSON, Ronald: *Emblem and Expression. Meaning in English Art of the Eighteenth Century,* Thames and Hudson, 1975.

PAULSON, Ronald: *Popular and Polite Art in the Age of Hogarth and Fielding,* University of Notre Dame Press, 1979.

## LIST OF ILLUSTRATIONS

*All paintings are by Hogarth unless otherwise identified.*

2 *The Shrimp Girl,* mid-1750s. Oil on canvas, 63.5 x 52.7 cm. Reproduced by courtesy of the Trustees, The National Gallery, London.

7 *Company of Undertakers,* 1736–7. Engraving, 21.9 x 17.8 cm. © British Museum.

8 Philippe Mercier, *The Music Party, Frederick, Prince of Wales and his Sisters, c.* 1733. Oil on canvas, 77.5 x 57.1 cm. © The National Trust, 1993, Cliveden House.

11 *Sir John Wilkes Esq,* 1763. Engraving, 31.7 x 22.2 cm. © British Museum.

12 *Sir Francis Dashwood at His Devotions,* mid-1750s. Oil on canvas, 121.9 x 88.9 cm. Private Collection.

15 *Characters and Caricatures,* 1743. Engraving, 19.5 x 20.6 cm. © British Museum.

16 Joseph Highmore, *Pamela and Mr. B in the Summer House, c.* 1744. Oil on canvas, 62.9 x 75.6 cm. Reproduction by permission of the Syndics of the Fitzwilliam Museum, Cambridge.

18 *Satire on False Perspective,* 1754. Engraving, 20.8 x 17.1 cm. © British Museum.

19 Paolo de Matteis, *The Choice of Hercules,* n.d. Oil on canvas, 198.2 x 256.5 cm. Ashmolean Museum, Oxford.

20 *A Harlot's Progress,* 1732. A series of six engravings, all approx. 11.5 x 14.5 cm. © British Museum.

24 *Industry and Idleness,* 1747. A series of twelve engravings, plates 1-10 incl. approx. 10.5 x 13.5 cm, plates 11 and 12 10.5 x 15.5 cm. © British Museum.

27 *Gin Lane,* 1750–51. Engraving, 36 x 30.5 cm. © British Museum.

29 *Time Smoking a Picture,* 1761. Engraving, 20.3 x 17 cm. © British Museum.

30 *Analysis of Beauty, Plate 1,* 1753. Engraving, 37.1 x 49 cm. © British Museum.

87 *Lord Hervey and His Friends, c.* 1738. Oil on canvas, 127 x 101 cm. © The National Trust, 1993, Ickworth House, Suffolk.

89 *Miss Mary Edwards, c.* 1740. Oil on canvas, 125.4 x 96.2 cm. © The Frick Collection, New York.

91 *Captain Thomas Coram,* 1740. Oil on canvas, 283.7 x 147.3 cm. The Thomas Coram Foundation for Children, London.

93 *The Graham Children,* 1742. Oil on canvas, 192.4 x 205 cm. Reproduced by courtesy of the Trustees, The National Gallery, London.

95 *The Country Dance, c.* 1745. Oil on canvas, 68.58 x 90.17 cm. Tate Gallery, London.

97 *David Garrick as Richard* III, 1745. Oil on canvas, 190.5 x 250 cm. Walker Art Gallery, Liverpool.

99 *Marriage à la Mode: 1. The Marriage Contract,* 1743–45. Oil on canvas, 69.9 x 90.8 cm. Reproduced by courtesy of the Trustees, The National Gallery, London.

101 *Marriage à la Mode: 2. Early in the Morning,* 1743–45. Oil on canvas, 69.9 x 90.8 cm. Reproduced by courtesy of the Trustees, The National Gallery, London.

103 *Marriage à la Mode: 3. The Inspection,* 1743–45. Oil on canvas, 69.9 x 90.8 cm. Reproduced by courtesy of the Trustees, The National Gallery, London.

105 *Marriage à la Mode: 4. The Toilette,* 1743–45. Oil on canvas, 70.5 x 90.8 cm. Reproduced by courtesy of the Trustees, The National Gallery, London.

107 *Marriage à la Mode: 5. The Death of the Earl,* 1743–45. Oil on canvas, 69.9 x 90.8 cm. Reproduced by courtesy of the Trustees, The National Gallery, London.

109 *Marriage à la Mode: 6. The Death of the Countess,* 1743–45. Oil on canvas, 69.9 x 90.8 cm. Reproduced by courtesy of the Trustees, The National Gallery, London.

111 *Self-Portrait with Pug,* 1745. Oil on canvas, 90 x 70 cm, Tate Gallery, London.

113 *Moses Brought before Pharaoh's Daughter,* 1746. Oil on canvas, 177.8 x 213.36 cm. The Thomas Coram Foundation for Children, London.

115 *Calais Gate, or O! The Roast Beef of England,* 1748. Oil on canvas, 78.94 x 95.6 cm. Tate Gallery, London.

117 *Paul before Felix,* 1748. Oil on canvas, 304.8 x 426.7 cm. Honourable Society of Lincoln's Inn, London.

119 *The March to Finchley,* 1749–50. Oil on canvas, 101.6 x 133.3 cm. The Thomas Coram Foundation for Children, London.

121 *An Election: 1. An Election Entertainment,* 1753–54. Oil on canvas, 101.6 x 127 cm. Sir John Soane's Museum, London.

123 *An Election: 2. Canvassing for Votes,* 1753–54. Oil on canvas, 101.6 x 127 cm. Sir John Soane's Museum, London.

125 *An Election: 3. The Polling,* 1753–54. Oil on canvas, 101.6 x 127 cm. Sir John Soane's Museum, London.

127 *An Election: 4. Chairing the Members,* 1753–54. Oil on canvas, 101.6 x 127 cm. Sir John Soane's Museum, London.

129 *Francis Matthew Schutz in his Bed,* 1755–60. Oil on canvas, 63 x 75.5 cm. Norfolk Museums Service (Norwich Castle Museum).

131 *Hogarth's Servants,* mid 1750–52. Oil on canvas, 62.23 x 75.56 cm. Tate Gallery, London.

133 *David Garrick and His Wife,* 1757. Oil on canvas, 17.4 x 18.1 cm. Windsor Castle, Royal Library. © 1993 Her Majesty The Queen.

135 *The Bench,* 1758. Oil on canvas, 17.4 x 18.1 cm. Reproduction by permission of the Syndics of The Fitzwilliam Museum, Cambridge.

137 *The Lady's Last Stake,* 1758–59. Oil on canvas, 91.44 x 105.41 cm. Albright Knox Art Gallery, Buffalo, New York, Gift of Seymour H. Knox, 1945.

139 *Sigismunda,* 1759. Oil on canvas, 99 x 125.73 cm. Tate Gallery, London.